BOOKS AUTHORED OR CO-AUTHORED
BY PAUL H. DUNN

You Too Can Teach

The Ten Most Wanted Men

Meaningful Living

Win If You Will

I Challenge You, I Promise You, Vol. 1

Discovering the Quality of Success

Relationships

Anxiously Engaged

The Osmonds

The Birth That We Call Death

Goals

You and Your World

Look at Your World

Life Planning

Dimensions of Life

I Challenge You, I Promise You, Vol. 2

Horizons

Your Eternal Choice

Success Is . . .

The Human Touch

Seek the Happy Life

Variable Clouds, Occasional Rain,
with a Promise of Sunshine

Mothers Need No Monuments

The Light of Liberty

Christmas: Do You Hear What I Hear?

After the Storm Comes
the Rainbow

No GREATER Gift

Understanding the Atonement of Jesus Christ

Paul H. Dunn

BOOKCRAFT
Salt Lake City, Utah

Library of Congress Catalog Card Number: 89-85675

ISBN 0-88494-691-6

Second Printing, 1989

Printed in the United States of America

Contents

Preface

Jesus Christ was and is the Son of God, our Heavenly Father, and is the Savior and Redeemer of mankind. He prepared the way by which, through the Atonement, we may be spared the everlasting separation of the body and spirit, have our sins forgiven, and be able to return once more into His presence.

We are not able to define or describe exactly how the process of redemption operates, but we can come to know the great eternal promise and blessing God has provided for us through Christ's atonement, the Father's greatest gift.

In this book I declare my own testimony and witness of Jesus Christ and His atonement. I would like to help instill in the minds of my readers the importance of His great mission and sacrifice, and the plan of salvation, and to teach how such knowledge can bring great peace and joy now and forever.

This book is not an official Church publication but represents the author's feelings and testimony of our Lord and Savior.

I am indebted to many for their assistance in the preparation of this work. Once more my wife, Jeanne, has performed an invaluable service in sharing thoughts and ideas and particularly her genius of expression. As a convert to the Church and having a strong Christian background, she has provided added insight into methods of sharing the gospel truths of which she has such a strong testimony.

To Sharene Hansen and Elaine Seaman, my able secretaries, I again express my gratitude and appreciation for their many talents and their devotion.

No volume of work such as this can be completed without acknowledgment being given to so many who, throughout the years, have written and borne testimony of our Lord and Savior. For the depth added to my own testimony from these valuable sources I am eternally grateful.

Introduction

Over the past many years, I have traveled to every state in our United States and to many countries of the world. It has been my wonderful privilege to visit and address marvelous congregations in all of these places, in many languages, and in many cultures. Prior to my call as a General Authority I taught for thirteen years thousands of high school and college youth on numerous campuses. Then came those wonderful years of sharing gospel truths with my missionaries and countless others as a mission president.

As exciting and important as these callings are and have been, my most sacred and vital of all assignments has been to teach my own children and grandchildren the eternal principles contained in the gospel of Jesus Christ. Together, my wife, Jeanne, and I have shared our knowledge, experience, and testimonies with each of these special individuals.

In previous books I have attempted to give some idea of my feelings and philosophy of life, not only to my posterity but to those everywhere who seek truth. I have written on subjects dealing with teaching, leadership, motivation, success, marriage, relationships, goals, patriotism, mothers, Christmas, death, overcoming fear, disappointment, and discouragement. As important as all these subjects might be, however, there is something even more vital that I wish to express here.

I was once asked, "If you were to deliver your last message on earth, what would you say?" This little volume contains, I believe, my answer to that question and what I would want my children and grandchildren to know, remember, and understand. It is my witness of the truthfulness of the gospel of Jesus Christ. Above all the counsel I would give or that which any parent or grandparent could give his family would be the testimony that God, the Father, is a reality, that He knows each of us and has abiding love for all of His children, and that He continually reveals Himself to us so that one day we can become like Him. I testify that His Son Jesus Christ, our Elder Brother, lives and is the Savior of the world, and that through Him the plan of salvation was instituted and found fulfillment. His atonement is the greatest event that has ever occurred on earth, and through His sacrifice all mankind will experience immortality and can work toward eternal life.

I join with my wife in declaring to my children and their children that Jesus Christ is the Son of the living God, our Father, and was crucified for the sins of mankind and that through Him we can all be reunited as an eternal family in that glorious day. In the pages that follow I share with you my most sincere feelings and testimony of that great truth.

CHAPTER 1

Once Upon a Time

Many hundreds of years ago, children living in the days of the Old and New Testaments and the Book of Mormon listened in awe to mighty stories and accounts of God and men. These very accounts, eventually becoming part of holy scripture, have been heard and appreciated by children through all generations of time with the same awe. All parts of the scriptures were and will always be the stuff drama is made of with their prophets and heroes, righteous and wicked kings, miracles, the terrible flood, the fiery destruction of cities, the clashing of armies, and great nations following their leaders into new and adventurous lands. As children have heard such stories through the ages, they have been more able to sense the deeper meaning of the scriptures as the living testimony of God and his concern for his offspring.

To illustrate, for a child full of questions about the world, eager to know how everything fits together, the story of the Creation could be tremendously exciting. I remember the experience of a little girl who, after having had a lesson on the book of Genesis in Primary one morning, realized for the first time that all she knew and had experienced about life had begun with the creation of heaven and earth. She raced home to break the news to her family, announcing, "Mommy, Daddy! Guess who made the world!"

Such experiences serve as building blocks toward the understanding and development of religious faith and best take place in an atmosphere where faith is lived and practiced, under the influence, first, of a loving family in the home, and then with dedicated Church teachers and leaders. It is important for us to remember that faith and trust aren't principles that are always just "taught" but are concepts that young people inescapably absorb through example in an environment where family members tend to talk aloud to the Lord at the dinner table and in their private prayers. There are also various times to learn about Him in gospel discussions within the family group. With religion as a part of daily life in home and Church-oriented situations, a child gradually develops an appreciation of the principle of faith—a feeling for what it is and what it can do.

We started this chapter by talking about stories. Have you ever noticed how many of them, including fairy tales, begin with those wonderful but simple words "Once upon a time"? I have made the interesting observation that often when a child hears those words, he enters another world where he is free to imagine whatever his heart desires. No movie, no video, no picture can begin to portray the scenes a child can paint in his own mind when he hears or reads "Once upon a time." There seems to be something magical in the phrase that allows those of any age to "stretch" the imagination— even the stories' authors do it—until it sometimes becomes difficult for us to separate what really is fact from what is fiction.

In my own life, during my growing-up years, this was a challenge to me. At one time I'm sure that I accepted the tale of "Snow White and the Seven Dwarfs" as pure fact until maturity eventually brought more profound reasonings. Then came the years during which I recognized that while my favorite sports stories contained much fact, they were also sprinkled with a great deal of fiction. I finally grew up enough to read and thoroughly enjoy *The Hunchback of Notre Dame,* and at that time I really believed the tale to be complete fiction. Even if those magic words, "Once upon a time," had been included at the beginning of the story, it wouldn't have been more of a fairy tale to me than it already was. Then later, to my surprise, I learned that the story was based on fact. Later still, while on a Church assignment in Paris, France, I toured the very cathedral where the story had taken place. My point is simple. Some stories are fiction but appear to be fact; some are fact but appear to be fairy tales. It takes some experience and time to tell the difference.

In that same vein, I have often thought that the most wonderful story I have ever read or told sounds like a fairy tale. It is the account of a man's life and mission and is so unique and uncommon that it could very well begin, "Once upon a time." It is the story of a perfect man. Now that fact alone makes it difficult for some to comprehend. But more than that it's about love and hate, life and death, and is so incredible that the reader must stop, think, and ponder carefully about it's contents. And still more is included in this almost unbelievable account. That is the equally amazing story, in all its many parts, of the environment and its accompanying circumstances in which He lived and functioned, and over which He presided as His mission commenced and over time, unfolded. And even a fairy tale would fall short of adequate and fitting words to convey the influence of that life and that environment and those circumstances on the lives of every one of us who has ever or will ever live.

Throughout all of the world's history there have been men of superior integrity and strength, exceptional accomplishment, and significant influence. In my own day and experience I have been deeply affected by many. I have always stood in awe of a David O. McKay, a Spencer W. Kimball, or an Ezra Taft Benson. On this earth there would be no one more remarkable in purpose, accomplishment, or profound contribution to society than a prophet of God. In another area of greatness, an area in which I have great interest, I have admired the courage of a Lou Gehrig, the thoughtfulness of a Babe Ruth, and the power of a Dale Murphy, all three of whom have exhibited outstanding strengths and skills. All of these men have distinguished themselves in their respective fields as very few could in this life. But as great as they are, the man of whom I now speak, Jesus the

Christ, far transcends in every virtue and strength, in every facet of His being and His life, anyone who has ever lived— He is unequaled in all of history.

As I have pondered the life, circumstances, and mission of our Savior, I have thought that Shakespeare missed a momentous opportunity in not using Jesus Christ as the theme of one of his great tragedies. But this life story that some would conclude had terminated tragically actually had the most magnificent of all endings, so magnificent that there is no possible way to adequately depict it; certainly no stage play, opera, or motion picture account could ever do it justice.

Because of the magnificence, the drama, the uncommonness of this, the greatest of all lives, it was natural that as we came to know and love and follow Him here in mortality, we would worship Him and find ways to celebrate His teachings, His virtues, and the important events of His life. Thus have come through all the ages our remembrances of the almost unbelievable and glorious beginning and end of His mortal life; His ministry, mission, and purpose; and His sacrifice for us. While traditionally we celebrate His birth and death separately as Christmas and Easter, in reality these two events should not be separated in our thinking. His birth would be meaningless without the understanding of its purpose, and His death, in all of its triumph, could not be fully appreciated without the inclusion of His miraculous and humble birth. And so we choose here to think of and refer to these two important occurrences as one in purpose, both being better understood and appreciated because of the other.

Whether at Christmastime, during the Easter season, or through every day of the year, we need to tell the greatest of all stories, that of Jesus' life and the series of steps and events that led to the fulfilling of His mission. I would like to do it in such a way that the scriptures will be "likened unto us," or, in other words, will have application in our lives. If the story of Jesus Christ were to remain a fairy tale, as it is to many, then the joy of its reality and truth would be lost.

As to format, this account might well begin, "Once upon a time." But unlike those wonderful fairy tales of our youth, it is my personal witness that the greatest story ever told is true.

CHAPTER 2

How Christmas
and Easter
Came to Be

My wife and I attended a World Series baseball game in California with some friends. The game was a great contest between two talented teams and great numbers of avid fans had turned out to watch it. Because the excited crowd numbered over fifty thousand, the noise was often almost deafening. People had to shout to be heard. As I sat there, I became very conscious of this huge mass of people, even a little awed by the fact that so many of us could be together in one place at the same time. Then I began to think of other large crowds I had been part of. Many times I have attended sporting and other types of events at the Rose Bowl in Pasadena, California, and at the Los Angeles Coliseum, both of which structures have seating capacities of over 100,000. I have enjoyed other contests at Soldier's Field in Chicago, where 110,000 people can be gathered. These crowds are always impressive. I remember on one of these occasions wondering what it would be like to sit with two hundred thousand soccer fans in the Maracana Stadium in Rio de Janeiro, Brazil. Can you imagine? No wonder Brazil seldom loses there! How would you like to be booed to defeat or cheered to victory in such an arena?

My point is to draw a comparison. While we marvel at the tremendous numbers of people that can assemble at these huge stadiums, you and I, although we don't remember, were once part of an even greater audience—greater than any ever gathered at an event held on earth. As a matter of fact, the gathering I refer to wasn't held on earth at all! It was part of our premortal experience, a meeting of all the billions of our Heavenly Father's children, and was the most important meeting we have ever attended. This experience was, in fact, the beginning of events that lead to our reasons for celebrating Christmas and Easter.

With all our imagination it would be impossible to grasp the magnitude of it all. Billions of us, and our Father knew each of us personally and loved us all. What a glorious thought!

To understand the assembly's purpose, it is important to know that we all lived in a premortal state of being in the presence of God our Father and that each of us had a spirit body. We were in His company, we saw Him, we knew Him, and we desired to become like Him. Every soul who lives or has ever lived has seen both the Father and the Son and has been in their presence in the spirit world.

To further explain this premortal existence, Elder Joseph Fielding Smith taught:

> When we lived in the presence of our Father, we were not like him, we were just spirits. We did not have bodies of flesh and bones but he did. He was a glorious personage with a body of flesh and bones, his spirit and body being inseparably connected, and his body shining with a brightness beyond the brightness of the sun. We saw him in His majesty. (*Church News*, May 31, 1947, p. 8.)

This premortal period was a wonderful state for us, but because not all of the experiences we needed to accomplish the Father's ultimate purposes for us could be obtained in that sphere, we were accorded the privilege of coming to an earth—a world planned, created, and prepared for our mortal existence.

The purpose of the enormous assembly, then, was for our Father's presentation to us of His proposal for the plan of our mortal birth into an earth life, or a human state. It was the plan of salvation, and all of us had the privilege of hearing it in its entirety and either accepting or rejecting it, which was consistent with the eternal nature of man's right and need of free agency. In this human condition, removed from our Father's presence, having forgotten all we had previously known and experienced, having received bodies of flesh and bone, continuing in the right and responsibility of individual choice—or free agency—and being governed by eternal law, we then could continue the progress our kind and wise Father desired for us.

Elder Smith adds further meaning:

> When the time arrived for us to be advanced in the scale of our existence and pass through this mundane probation [earth life], councils were held and the spirit children were instructed in matters pertaining to conditions in mortal life, and the reason for such an existence. In the former life we were spirits. In order that we should advance and eventually gain the goal of perfection, it was made known that we would receive tabernacles of flesh and bones and have to pass through mortality where we would be tried and proved to see if we, by trial, would prepare ourselves for exaltation. (*Church News,* June 12, 1949, p. 21.)

He also taught:

> When the plan of salvation was presented to us, it was made known to us that if we would pass through this mortal existence, and be true and faithful to all the commandments our Father would give unto us, thus keeping the second estate as we had kept the first [premortal life], we too eventually would have the privilege of coming back into his presence with bodies of flesh and bones which would also shine with the brightness of the sun, to share in all the fulness of his kingdom (*Church News*, May 31, 1947, p. 8).

As we picture the billions of our Father's children gathered there, we can only wonder and marvel at the method used to make it possible for so vast an assemblage to hear—undoubtedly something more sophisticated than the microphones and televisions we know today. But we did hear—and observe—all that happened at that marvelous meeting.

At this point I am reminded of an experience I have heard my father talk about many times. During the era of his youth, spent in Provo, Utah, the radio was not as yet being used widely, and the television had not even been invented. Public communication at the time was difficult at best.

He tells about attending his deacons quorum meeting one Sunday morning, the lesson for the day being on the premortal Council in Heaven. The quorum teacher related how all Heavenly Father's children were assembled together to hear the plan of salvation and how, upon hearing from God Himself the events to come, they were filled with happiness and shouted for joy!

This apparently made quite an impression on my father, who at that time was twelve years old, and after class he rushed home to discuss it with his mother. He had been intrigued with the whole account of the council and the huge gathering and the fact that even he himself had been there. For a few minutes he went on excitedly telling his mother about the lesson. Finally he stopped and, with a very questioning look on his face, said, "There's only one thing I really don't understand." His mother looked at him and asked, "What's that, Harold?" "How could it all be true?" my father replied. "How could God talk to all those people at once so that they could hear Him when I can't even hear what the bishop is saying past the middle of the Provo Tabernacle?"

I have often wondered what my father would have thought at that tender age had his mother been able to say to him, "Harold, someday after you've grown up and married Geneve Roberts, you will have three sons. One of those sons, Paul, will be called as a General Authority of the Church and will stand at the pulpit of the Salt Lake Tabernacle and address millions of people the world over—all at once!"

As we recognize the many scientific advances that have been made since my father's childhood, it is interesting to contemplate what was and is yet possible in Heavenly Father's scope.

Now back to our own account of the vast assembly. Yes, we did hear, and as we listened we learned vital and beautiful truth and knowledge.

Along with an earth for our inheritance, the plan provided for two of the Father's choicest spirits, Adam and Eve, to become the parents of the human race and for their changing from an immortal state into one which would subject them to mortality, thus enabling them to perform their vital mission.

Our lives would be purposeful and would be a time of mortal probation, a testing period. During this time we would have the opportunity to learn and to live divine principles and to realize the possibility of our Godlike potential by the things we might accomplish, the fulfilling relationships we might develop and sustain, and the wise choices we might make. We would continue to exercise our eternal blessing of agency; we would be confronted with the challenge of opposition — the knowledge and experience of both good and evil, and the discovery of joy as opposed to what we would suffer. The plan indeed contained the *promise* of happiness despite our struggle, weakness, frustrations, and aches and pains.

We heard that all of Heavenly Father's creations would be eternal, that they would be on-going and have meaning and purpose, and that His plan for each of us would be to develop our individual personalities, to enlarge our souls, and to become like Him:

> For behold, this is my work and my glory—to bring to pass the immortality and eternal life of man (Moses 1:39).

Finally, physical death would occur, followed by life after death. We would have hope for the future and a glorious resurrection, which would be brought about through the atonement of His Only Begotten Son, Jesus Christ.

Our modern-day scriptures have given us additional insight into the important events of that meeting, which was called the Council in Heaven. Not only did we learn the pur-

pose of our lives but also the nature of the Godhead and our
relationship to God and our elder brother, Jesus Christ. The
most valuable teaching we received and the greatest event
that occurred at the council concerned Christ, who was present along with us and who had not yet entered mortality Himself. It was at this time that He was chosen by His Father and
delegated with the power to initiate and carry out the glorious plan of salvation under His Father's direction and commandment.

God's selection of Christ, in whom He entrusted the leadership of His great work, was not, however, without conflict
on the part of another of His sons, Lucifer. In a revelation
from the Eternal Father to Moses, the account of this great
event is given:

> And I, the Lord God, spake unto Moses, saying: That
> Satan, whom thou hast commanded in the name of mine
> Only Begotten, is the same which was from the beginning,
> and he came before me, saying—Behold, here am I, send me,
> I will be thy son, and I will redeem all mankind, that one
> soul shall not be lost, and surely I will do it; wherefore give
> me thine honor.
>
> But, behold, my Beloved Son, which was my Beloved and
> Chosen from the beginning, said unto me—Father, thy will
> be done, and the glory be thine forever. (Moses 4:1–2.)

In response to the above passage Orson Whitney penned
these words:

> He spake;—attention grew more grave,
> The stillness e'en more still.
>
> "Father!"—the voice like music fell, . . .
> "Father," it said, "since one must die,
>   Thy children to redeem,
> Whilst earth, as yet unformed and void,
> Where pulsing life shall teem;

> And thou, great Michael, foremost fall,
>   that mortal man may be;
> And chosen Saviour yet must send,
>   Lo, here am I—send me!
>
> I ask, I seek no recompense,
>   Save that which then were mine;
> Mine be the willing sacrifice,
>   The endless glory, thine!"

("Elect of Elohim," *Elias—An Epoch of the Ages* [New York: Knickerbacher Press, 1904], p. 31.)

To continue the scriptural account:

> Wherefore, because that Satan rebelled against me, and sought to destroy the agency of man, which I, the Lord God, had given him, and also, that I should give unto him mine own power; by the power of mine Only Begotten, I caused that he should be cast down;
> And he became Satan, yea, even the devil, the father of all lies, to deceive and to blind men, and to lead them captive at his will, even as many as would not hearken unto my voice (Moses 4:3–4).

President David O. McKay gives us some valuable insight into the above scripture:

> Two things you will note in that passage: one, that Satan was determined to destroy the free agency of man. Free agency is a gift of God. It is a part of his divinity. The second point is that he desired to supplant God. I quote, "Give me thine glory."

President McKay continues to point out that:

> The world does not comprehend the significance of that divine gift to the individual. It is as inherent as intelligence which, we are told, has never been nor can be created. . . .

A fundamental principle of the gospel is free agency, and references in the scriptures show that this principle is (1) essential to man's salvation; and (2) may become a measuring rod by which the actions of men, of organizations, of nations may be judged.

"Therefore," we are told in the scripture, "cheer up your hearts, and remember that ye are free to act for yourselves — to choose the way of everlasting death or the way of eternal life." (2 Nephi 10:23.) . . .

. . . It is the impelling source of the soul's progress. It is the purpose of the Lord that man becomes like him. In order for man to achieve this, it was necessary for the Creator first to make him free. To man is given a special endowment, not bestowed upon any other living thing. God gave him the power of choice. Only to the human being did the Creator say: ". . . thou mayest choose for thyself, for it is given unto thee; . . ." (Moses 3:17.) Without this divine power to choose, humanity cannot progress. (In Conference Report, October 1965, pp. 7–8.)

We know from the scriptures that Jesus had a unique role as the supervisor of the divinely formulated plan, a role that had many facets. Among other things, He was to be the organizer — the Creator — of our world and many other worlds. Heavenly Father revealed to Moses this fact:

> And worlds without number have I created; and I also created them for mine own purpose; and by the Son I created them, which is mine Only Begotten (Moses 1:33).

Jesus, under the Father's direction, was also to place man on the earth, to guide humanity until they should return to the spirit world, and become man's Savior and Redeemer by restoring his perfected mortal body to his eternal spirit, bringing him back to God, and atoning for human error. Thus He became, in all matters pertaining to the earth and humanity, the official representative of our Father in Heaven, directly in charge of all affairs and people on earth.

In recognition of Jesus' appointment, the plan of salvation with its body of truths, principles, and laws is called the gospel of Jesus Christ, and for that reason also we pray to the Father in the name of His Son Jesus Christ. This is the reason, too, that our church is called The Church of Jesus Christ of Latter-day Saints.

We have all seen some great dramas in life, but there are few things that will ever compare with that majestic scene of the Council in Heaven in our permortal home. The decision was made: not only did most of us accept the plan of mortality but in addition our Beloved Brother was to be our Redeemer. And, at the same time, that great antagonist, Satan himself, was cast out. No wonder the scriptures testify that "the morning stars sang together, and all the sons of God shouted for joy" (Job 38:7)!

I suppose many of us have observed at some time a hundred thousand frenzied men and women yelling in unison in an earthly stadium, but I believe that the shout of joy that went up as our Brother took His place at our Father's side must have reverberated throughout every corner of the heavens. Again, it was the beginning of events leading to our celebrations of the real meaning of Christmas and Easter.

A knowledge of the premortal existence of mankind and the beginning of the gospel as the true plan of salvation is taught with great clearness in scripture.

> And thus the Gospel began to be preached, from the beginning, being declared by holy angels sent forth from the presence of God, and by his own voice, and by the gift of the Holy Ghost.
>
> And thus all things were confirmed unto Adam, by an holy ordinance, and the Gospel preached, and a decree sent forth, that it should be in the world, until the end thereof; and thus it was. Amen. (Moses 5:58–59.)
>
> And our father Adam spake unto the Lord, and said: Why is it that men must repent and be baptized in water? And the Lord said unto Adam: Behold I have forgiven thee thy transgression in the Garden of Eden.
>
> Hence came the saying abroad among the people, that the Son of God hath atoned for original guilt, wherein the sins of

the parents cannot be answered upon the heads of the children, for they are whole from the foundation of the world. (Moses 6:53–54.)

And Enoch continued his preaching in righteousness unto the people of God. And it came to pass in his days, that he built a city that was called the City of Holiness, even Zion. (Moses 7:19.)

A statement of the reality of the resurrection and immortality is also given:

And righteousness will I send down out of heaven; and truth will I send forth out of the earth, to bear testimony of mine Only Begotten; his resurrection from the dead; yea, and also the resurrection of all men; and righteousness and truth will I cause to sweep the earth as with a flood, to gather out mine elect from the four quarters of the earth, unto a place which I shall prepare, an Holy City, that my people may gird up their loins, and be looking forth for the time of my coming, for there shall be my tabernacle, and it shall be called Zion, a New Jerusalem (Moses 7:62).

What the scriptures have taught and testified to is real, not only to me but also to hundreds of thousands of witnesses—men, women, and children—who have received an assurance of the reality of the spirit world. Just as surely as we live now, there was and is a premortal life, and, though it was not meant that we remember all of our life there, I am certain that many of us have experienced, at some time or other, a sort of flashback to places and situations which, though real and familiar, we are not conscious of having seen or been a part of previously.

This happened to me once during World War II as I was on a patrol in the jungles of the Philippines where the enemy abounded all around us. The brush was thick and the palm trees plentiful. Often the enemy soldiers would conceal themselves in the underbrush or trees, waiting for the appropriate moment to attack. I had never been in the Philippine Islands in my young life prior to landing there as a member of the U.S. Army Infantry.

All of a sudden our patrol burst into an open clearing in the landscape and there before me was a scene with which I was very familiar. Had I been blindfolded, I could have described every part of the terrain that lay before me. I recall thinking, "I have seen this place or I have been here before!" Perhaps for just a moment the veil of the premortal past had been lifted.

Such occurrences and testimonies have been experienced even by the very young. Some time ago I read of such an account:

"I had always heard that one could learn many things from children, but not until we had a very precious experience with one of our own did I realize how true this could be.

"This occasion took place when our first child, Alan, was just past two. Alan had learned to talk very early, so by this time he spoke very clearly and could express himself with a sizeable vocabulary for his age.

"Alan's great-aunt, Lida, had just passed away; and I had been worrying about how I was going to tell him about 'death.' We had taken him to see her once or twice a week, so there had to be some explanation for the termination of our visits.

"Mustering all my courage, for I was new at that sort of thing then, I sat Alan on the kitchen stool and drew up a chair. 'Alan, Honey,' I said, 'Aunt Lida has gone back to Heavenly Father.'

"But, before I could say anything more, he asked, 'Who took her?' I stumbled around for an answer, and then I said, 'It must have been someone she knew.'

"Immediately his little face lit up as if he recognized a familiar situation. He said with a happy smile, 'Oh, I know what it's like! Grandpa Clark brought me when I came to you. He'll probably take me back when I die.'

"Alan then proceeded to describe his Grandfather Clark, my father, who had been dead nearly twelve years. He had never even seen a picture of him. He told me how much he loved his grandfather and how good he had been to him. He indicated that my father had helped to teach him and prepare him to come here. He also spoke of Heavenly Father as a definite memory.

"Needless to say, this little conversation with Alan that I had been dreading turned out to be one of the sweetest experiences of my life. It left me limp with humility and joy. I no longer felt sorry that my father could not see my children. As each little soul has come along, I have felt that my father probably was better acquainted with the newcomer than was I. This has been a great comfort to me.

"Immediately after this occasion, Alan's father talked to him; and Alan repeated the same answers to him. He later told the experience to his Grandmother Clark. For several months he talked about these things as a happy, natural memory of real experiences. Then, suddenly, the memory was erased and he did not know what we were talking about when we discussed it." (Betty Clark Ruff, *Instructor*, 1963.)

What a marvelous experience! The history of our premortal existence is fact! It is just as Wordsworth stated:

> Our birth is but a sleep and a forgetting:
> The Soul that rises with us, our life's Star,
> Hath had elsewhere its setting,
> And cometh from afar:
> Not in entire forgetfulness,
> And not in utter nakedness,
> But trailing clouds of glory do we come
> From God, who is our home.
> (William Wordsworth, *Ode: Intimations of Immortality from Recollections of Early Childhood.*)

It is also just as Plato records in *Phaedo:*

> Your favorite doctrine, Socrates, that knowledge is simply recollection, if true, also necessarily implies a previous time in which we have learned that which we now recollect. But

this would be impossible unless our soul had been in some place before existing in the form of man; here then is another proof of the soul's immortality. (Robert Maynard Hutchings, *Great Books of the Western World.*)

These are merely additional witnesses obviously prompted by the Light of Christ that testify of our eternal existence. And with those witnesses comes a stronger assurance that the true meaning of Christmas and Easter really began years ago in that great council. It is just as the scriptures themselves verify: Christ was truly foreordained to be the Savior from the foundations of the world (John 3:16).

I submit that looking at Christ and His sacrifice in light of the whole plan of salvation will allow us increased appreciation and love for the Savior. It will make our feelings at Christmas and Easter more powerful and pure and we will remember that those special days had their beginning "Once upon a time in a far away place."

CHAPTER 3

Truth
and
Consequences

For centuries the story of man and his life has been for many a great mystery. Millions have wondered and still do, "from whence do we come?" "Why are we here?" "Did a person named Jesus Christ really live, and if so, was he a Son of God?" "For that matter, is there really a God at all, and who and what and where is He?"

To some, man has evolved from a lower form of life or was an accident. To others he is God's greatest creation because of a divine plan. Science and religion have long been at odds over these points, and the question still looms as to the age of man and the earth—whether that age is billions or thousands of years old. However, it is not the intent of this book to debate the issue of science and religion but to explain my feelings and understandings of the Atonement, God's greatest gift to man through His Son Jesus Christ.

I have learned through years of teaching young people that to get the full perspective and appreciation of this great event and process, it is valuable to look at the Atonement, not just as a lone topic, but as part of a larger, all-encompassing whole made up of many individual parts, somewhat like a gigantic jigsaw puzzle. And like any puzzle, the entire picture, including all its views, cannot be fully understood or enjoyed until all the pieces are in place together.

In this effort to portray the Atonement then, the "whole" subject—the plan of salvation—has been presented, showing how all the parts fit together to make the Atonement what it is. Here, another word of explanation. It has long been my feeling, especially working with young people, that one of the most confusing aspects of teaching and learning, in fact just plain living, is the semantics of our language, our understanding of the meanings of various words and terms. As teachers, or as any of us, try to express our thoughts, concepts, and points of view, we all do so in our own individual styles, using certain words and phrases that to us best describe or define that which we are trying to communicate. And, too, we all automatically picture in our minds, according to our own experiences and understanding, the various objects or ideas that are presented to us. In other words, people simply don't think, see, and communicate things in the same way. For example, if, in a conversation with you, I mentioned dogs, your mind would picture certain kinds of dogs and I would undoubtedly think of other kinds. So it is when explaining concepts.

In keeping with the subject of our text, think of the words *immortality, eternal life,* and *salvation.* Occasionally there is confusion over the actual meaning of these terms because they are often used interchangeably—one writer, speaker, or teacher using them to define one thing, and another, something else. For our purpose here, the word *immortality* will be used to mean life, through the resurrection, which will last forever. *Eternal life* is life in exaltation, or the celestial kingdom. The term *salvation* has been used over the years by writers and speakers to mean at least three different things: man saved from temporal death; man saved from his sins; or the saving of man from both of these—in other words, the whole of the Atonement. In the expression *the plan of salvation,* for example, the term *salvation* means man's complete redemption, or being saved from both temporal and spiritual death and being saved from his sins. Any other usage I would make of the term *salvation*, unless otherwise explained, would refer solely to the resurrection.

Then there are in the scriptures the many titles for Deity, always very accurate in describing the personages intended but nevertheless confusing. Who is actually being referred to at a given time? These titles can rightly be and certainly are used interchangeably many times, sometimes causing us to misinterpret the verses of scripture we are reading.

There are other scriptural terms that are often puzzling to us. For example, such a phrase as "suffer them to come" really means "let them or allow them to come."

I am sensitive to these concerns to the point that throughout the text I will attempt wherever practical to lend some necessary understanding.

In the preceding chapter, we discussed the first steps of the plan of salvation: the premortal life, the Council in Heaven, and the calling of our Savior, Jesus Christ, by His Father to the very important role He was to play in the scheme of things.

The plan that God the Father had presented to us in the spirit world and which we accepted at that time had been masterfully, brilliantly put together in perfect detail and in complete accordance with eternal law to provide for every need of mankind. Each step or phase fit together exactly as only the most supreme intelligence could conceive it. Every provision had been made for the attainment of the father's ultimate goal for His children. Now we were able to fully realize that Jesus Christ's entire life — in the premortal spirit world, in mortality, and in postmortal life as well — was to be devoted to bringing about that goal, under the direction of the Father.

Now as Christ assumed His role as executor of the plan of salvation, one of the many instructions given Him by His father was that recorded in Moses 2:26–27.

> And I, God, said unto mine Only Begotten, which was with me from the beginning: Let us make man in our image, after our likeness; and it was so. And I, God, said: Let them have dominion over the fishes of the sea, and over the fowl of the air, and over the cattle, and over all the earth, and over every creeping thing that creepeth upon the earth.

> And I, God, created man in mine own image, in the image of mine Only Begotten created I him; male and female created I them.

And, of course, the male and female He created were Adam and Eve. In the spirit world, they had been called and had willingly accepted the role and responsibility, with its sacrifice, of becoming the earthly parents of the human race, of starting the process of peopling the earth, which was one of the vital steps of the overall plan.

In a great part of the Christian world there has always been much confusion about the story of the creation of the earth and our first parents, much doubt of its truthfulness. Some religious faiths have come to discredit the account all together, considering it nothing more than a myth. Some hold the opinion that Adam and Eve, though originally created in a state of grace, committed a serious sin by disobeying God's commandment in the Garden of Eden and, therefore, fell out of favor with their Father. God, then, in anger, alienated Himself from Adam and Eve and banished them from the Garden and His presence.

There is also a notion in some Christian thought that when they "fell," through sin, called the original sin, all of their posterity became sinners also. Man himself, therefore, was depraved and evil by nature and would remain so until God, through Christ's atonement, would restore him once again to a state of grace and redeem him from death and sin.

The Church of Jesus Christ of Latter-day Saints takes a different position. We learn from the scriptures that as part of the Father's instruction to Adam and Eve in the Garden of Eden, He gave them two commandments which were in opposition to each other. One was to multiply and replenish the earth:

> And I, God, blessed them, and said unto them: Be fruitful, and multiply, and replenish the earth, and subdue it, and have dominion over the fish of the sea, and over the fowl of the air, and over every living thing that moveth upon the earth (Moses 2:28).

This meant they must *eat* of the tree of the knowledge of good and evil so that they would become mortal and get understanding.

The other commandment, directly opposite of the first, was that they *not eat* of the tree of the knowledge of good and evil.

> And I, the Lord God, commanded the man, saying: Of every tree of the garden thou mayest freely eat [including the tree of life which would bring immortal life],
>
> But of the tree of the knowledge of good and evil, thou shalt not eat of it, nevertheless, thou mayest choose for thyself, for it is given unto thee; but, remember that I forbid it, for in the day thou eatest thereof thou shalt surely die [temporal, physical death and mortality]. (Moses 3:16–17.)

It would seem that they must have been in a real quandary. Both commandments could not be obeyed as they were directly opposed to each other. In order to multiply and replenish the earth, Adam and Eve, themselves, would have to become mortal, to experience mortal life and physical death, and to be subject to opposition—good and evil, joy and sorrow—all of which would be possible only by eating the forbidden fruit. To have chosen obedience to the second commandment would have meant that they remain the way they were, immortal, and therefore unable to beget mortal children. Thus the Father's plan would have been thwarted. We know that from the beginning it was meant that they and *we* go through life and death in mortality; but, nevertheless, in the garden God gave them the opportunity, the right—in fact it was a necessity—to choose for themselves. Surely coming as no surprise to the Father, they chose mortality with its accompanying hardships, and though there had been some forgetting, there must also have been knowledge and understanding sufficient to make the decision possible.

The act is known, of course, as the fall of Adam and, as previously mentioned, is considered by many to have been an awful transgression, an act of great disobedience on the part of Adam and Eve and, as such, carries a very negative and sinful connotation.

We believe that Adam was not in any way a sinner but rather was a responsible, dedicated agent of God the Father, understanding his own purposes and accepting the resulting consequences, both good and bad.

The Book of Mormon teaches the optimistic and true meaning of the Fall:

> And now, behold, if Adam had not transgressed he would not have fallen, but he would have remained in the garden of Eden. And all things which were created must have remained in the same state in which they were after they were created; and they must have remained forever, and had no end.
>
> And they would have had no children; wherefore they would have remained in a state of innocence, having no joy, for they knew no misery; doing no good, for they knew no sin.
>
> But behold, all things have been done in the wisdom of him who knoweth all things.   ·
>
> Adam fell that men might be; and men are, that they might have joy. (2 Nephi 2:22–25.)

Other revelations also reject the concept of original sin. Alma tells us:

> And now behold, I say unto you that if it had been possible for Adam to have partaken of the fruit of the *tree of life* at that time, there would have been no death, and the word would have been void, making God a liar, for he said: If thou eat thou shalt surely die.
>
> And we see that death comes upon mankind, yea, the death which has been spoken of by Amulek, which is the temporal death; nevertheless there was a space granted unto man in which he might repent; therefore this life became a probationary [testing] state; a time to prepare to meet God; a time to prepare for that endless state which has been spoken of by us, which is after the resurrection of the dead. . . .
>
> And now behold, if it were possible that our first parents could have gone forth and partaken of the *tree of life* they

would have been forever miserable, having no preparatory state; and thus the plan of redemption would have been frustrated, and the word of God would have been void, taking none effect. (Alma 12:23–24, 26; italics added.)

And in Moses we read:

And in that day Adam blessed [was grateful to] God and was filled, and began to prophesy concerning all the families of the earth, saying: Blessed be the name of God, for because of my transgression my eyes are opened, and in this life I shall have joy, and again in the flesh I shall see God.

And Eve, his wife, heard all these things and was glad, saying: Were it not for our transgression we never should have had seed, and never should have known good and evil, and the joy of our redemption, and the eternal life which God giveth unto all the obedient. (Moses 5:10–11.)

Seeing in the Fall good results for Adam and Eve and all of humanity, President John Taylor said:

They would have been incapable of increase; and without that increase the designs of God in relation to the formation of the earth and man could not have been accomplished; for one great object of the creation of the world was the propagation [reproduction] of the human species, that bodies might be prepared for those spirits who already existed and who, when they saw the earth formed, shouted for joy (*The Gospel Kingdom* [Salt Lake City: Bookcraft, 1987], p. 96).

Apostle John A. Widtsoe explains:

Though a command had been given, Adam was permitted to exercise his free agency. "Thou mayest choose for thyself." The eternal power of choice was respected by the Lord himself. That throws a flood of light on the "Fall." It really converts the command into a warning, as much as if to say, if you do this thing, you will bring upon yourself a certain punishment [consequence]; but do it if you choose.

And he goes on:

> Satan . . . seeks to overthrow the work of God. By induc-
> ing Adam and Eve to disobey the Lord, he thought to have
> them in his power. He forgot, or did not know, that by their
> very "disobedience" the purposes of the Lord with respect
> to his spirit children would be accomplished. The temptation
> of Eve turned upon him to the defeat of his evil designs. . . .
>
> Considering our full knowledge of the purpose of the
> plan of salvation, and the reason for placing Adam and Eve
> on earth, the apparent contradiction in the story of the "Fall"
> vanishes. Instead the law of free agency, or individual choice,
> appears in distinct view. (*Evidences and Reconciliations* [Salt
> Lake City: Bookcraft, 1987], pp. 193, 195.)

It might be said that the Fall was actually a means of intro-
ducing the principle of free agency into mortal existence. At
the very least, the great true-life drama of Adam and Eve
teaches us in a deeply meaningful way of the importance and
blessing of this tremendous principle in man's life.

It has previously been stated, as we have proceeded
through these pages, that our purpose is to define and discuss
the various steps leading to mankind's final goal and blessing
—his attainment of immortality and eternal life. Any study of
these subjects exposes us frequently to the phrase "the demands of justice." These words, found throughout all of
scripture, in many of the writings of the prophets, and, in
general, through all of Christian history, are so significant to
our progress toward our goal and so essential to our understanding of the plan of salvation that it seems appropriate to
turn our attention to them for a moment. They represent the
very fundamental truth and reality of eternal law, which has
unique and important attributes. If these attributes are understood they can help us to govern our lives more satisfactorily
here on earth and can give us greater assurance of happiness
and attainment in our postmortal lives. I will attempt to give a
brief explanation of some of them in the following para-
graphs.

The purpose of eternal law is to produce and maintain order and continuity in every aspect of life. In some way which we don't yet fully understand, law carries with it tremendous strength, power, and control over all of existence. Unless we function in harmony with that power and control, our lack of compliance becomes the source of great unhappiness, suffering, and even tragedy here on earth and as those effects are felt even in life after death.

As Latter-day Saints, we believe that eternal, unchanging law, or to use another term, justice, is the governing force of every phase of existence. Even God the Supreme Being respects and honors this truth and lives and functions in accordance with all law. He is not above law Himself, but is bound by it, in spite of all His knowledge and power.

We believe that there is a law that makes possible the organization and function of everything, even the most minute particle of matter, either animate or inanimate. It governs every action and every thought. Nothing is created or functions or is performed successfully without having been controlled by the process of law and order. Thus in life, there are millions of laws, billions of laws, any or all of which could affect us if they come into our experience.

In giving definition to the nature and attributes of eternal law we could well use words such as *unbendable, invariable, inflexible, unchanging, demanding, rigid, absolute, unyielding, fixed, inviolable, impartial.* From this description perhaps one can get a clearer picture of the phrase earlier mentioned, "the demands of justice." Other ways to simply state this thought or phrase are "the strictness of law," or "law is unbending," or "there's no way to get around it."

The next attribute is that of cause and effect, or to put it another way, truth or consequences.

When I was in high school one of the most popular radio programs on the air was a game show called *Truth or Consequences.* It was so well liked and had such a following that eventually it was carried on into television and ran for some years with equal popularity there.

The point of the game was that contestants were called out of the audience and asked various questions. If they answered the questions correctly they were given certain rewards. However, if they failed to give the appropriate answers, they were called upon to participate in some very humorous, though often embarrassing, situations as their consequences. Much of the time they failed to answer properly, thus the program was often humorous—at the expense of the contestants, of course.

In a very real sense the game of life has a similar format. Like the various game show questions that called for particular, definite answers, life is subject to certain conditions or principles that call for very particular, very definite responses. If those responses are not given, certain effects inescapably follow. Unlike the game show, however, not all of those effects will be humorous—in fact, many will be just the opposite.

These conditions to which we are subject are, of course, eternal laws, and every law, every truth, has a natural consequence or effect or result that comes to us, a positive effect if the law is strictly followed or a negative effect if it is not. Therefore:

—If a child runs into the street and is directly hit by a speeding car, he can be either killed or injured.

—If you drop a book out of a fourth story window, it will, unless stopped by another force, fall to the ground because of the law of gravity.

—If a baseball is thrown at a glass windowpane, the weight and speed of the traveling ball will cause it, unless stopped in another way, to shatter the glass because of other scientific laws (a fact I have had proven to me many times over during my baseball playing days).

—If you choose to fill up your car's gas tank with water from the garden hose, your car will not take you very far (as witnessed by one of our daughters who, driving her car under those exact circumstances, managed the distance to the school, where she dropped off her five-year-old son, the culprit, and then got only halfway home. She then had to walk, in bathrobe and bare feet, two blocks for help. I am sure you can read into this that the walk in bathrobe and bare feet was a consequence of other interesting choices.)

— Likewise, applying the Golden Rule as an example of a moral law—by showing love and concern, unselfishness and kindness towards others, we will accomplish things in relationships that indifference, intolerance, and self-centeredness never could.

Interestingly, because of the unyielding nature of law (justice) we sometimes find ourselves feeling discomfort, or worse, from breaking a law we weren't even aware we had broken. From this we can see that ignorance of a truth doesn't keep us from the natural result or consequence of our actions. The law is no respecter of persons or circumstances.

We must also realize that all eternal law, all truth (as opposed to theory) will remain unchanged and will not in any way be affected by our lack of understanding and acceptance of it and will eventually be proven by its results.

Before leaving law's attributes, I add these thoughts. There are three kinds or categories of law which are often referred to and which, for the sake of understanding, should, to me, be differentiated between: eternal law, God's law, and man-made law. The purpose of all three is the same, to establish and keep order and to become standards against which to judge or measure performance.

Eternal law, as already stated, is perfect and complete truth and never changes in its format. It has existed and will continue to exist unchanged forever. And there is a difference between law and theory, theory being those thoughts and processes that are steps toward recognizing eternal law.

God's law—divine or spiritual law—referred to so often in both the scriptures and other religious writings, is, to me, actually eternal law itself because God is a God of law and follows and respects nothing out of harmony with perfect truth. Thus, it would seem inconsistent that He would give us anything but that to which He submits Himself. This definition is given here to help readers avoid confusion wherever these two terms, eternal law and God's law, might be encountered.

Man-made law is formulated to meet the needs and conditions relative to individuals and their earthly societies. These laws work to protect our free agency and our safety as we live and function in these societies. But because man-made laws are based on man's finite, thus limited, knowledge and understanding, they are often inconsistent with eternal law, though we are bound by them to the extent of great loss of freedom when we disobey them.

Personal knowledge of the reality of law and its natural consequences has motivated many to attest to these facts in writing, in the scriptures, as well as in other avenues. Here are a few examples of human experience and thought:

— You reap what you sow.
— Remote or near, the universe is under a reign of law.
— If something is done, a definite result follows. If something is desired, some definite things must be done.
— In the heavens above, as in the earth below, law prevails.
— He hath given a law unto all things by which they move in their times and their seasons, and their courses are fixed.
— Spiritual law, binding upon man, if he desires certain blessings, has been repeatedly set forth in sacred writ.
— The greatest sufferings of the world may be traced to the unholy, destructive doctrine that man need not conform to law, whether of man, nature, or God.
— None shall be exempt from the justice and the laws of God that all things may be done in order.
— Recognize the law, conform to it, obey it, and the law helps, never hinders.
— The ultimate result of good deeds is happiness, the consequence of evil is misery; these follow in every man's life by invisible law.

And finally:
> — There is a law, irrevocably decreed in heaven before
> the foundations of this world, upon which all bless-
> ings [positive consequences] are predicated—And
> when we obtain any blessing from God, it is by obe-
> dience to that law upon which it is predicated (D&C
> 130:20–21).

The consequences of going contrary to true principles is
vividly portrayed in this true story:

Robert Scott, the famed British explorer, while on his return from his expedition to the South Pole, ran out of food,
and on March 29, 1912, he and his last two surviving companions died. Several months later when their frozen bodies were
discovered, Scott's diaries were found and his final message
to the world read:

"The causes of the disaster are not due to faulty organisation, but to misfortune in all risks which had to be undertaken. . . . We are weak, writing is difficult, but for my own
sake I do not regret this journey, which has shown that En-
glishmen can endure hardships, help one another, and meet
death with as great a fortitude as ever in the past. We took
risks, we knew we took them; things have come out against
us, and therefore we have no cause for complaint, but bow to
the will of Providence, determined still to do our best to the
last. . . . Had we lived, I should have had a tale to tell of the
hardihood, endurance, and courage of my companions
which would have stirred the heart of every Englishman.
These rough notes and our dead bodies must tell the tale, but
surely, surely, a great rich country like ours will see that those
who are dependent on us are properly provided for."

The image of Robert Scott and his last message over the
years has placed him among the heroes of twentieth-century
scientific exploration circles. However, years later it now ap-
pears that Scott died because of his repeated failures in judgment and leadership.

Jared Diamond, a noted explorer of the New Guinea
jungles, pointed out that "as long as the conventional view of

Scott persisted, his death could teach us nothing. . . . But now, [with new insight and information surrounding Scott's tragedy] . . . , there are much broader lessons for all of us, lessons about calculating risks, motivating people, and accepting responsibility for our own mistakes. Those lessons become more vivid when the penalty for not learning them is death in an antarctic wasteland." Such experiences provide a parable for life itself.

Diamond further says that "Scott's diaries reveal a regular failure to provide margins of safety." He recalls that "Scott ran out of supplies and died just 11 miles short of his One Ton Depot. That depot's location had resulted from dozens of decisions; correcting any one of them would have placed the depot nearer to the Pole and thus saved Scott." He gives four examples:

"On February 17, 1911, Titus Oates, who was helping Scott set up the depot, urged him to take the four strongest ponies and proceed farther before caching the supplies. Scott refused, saying, 'I'm not going to defy my feelings for the sake of a few days' march.'

"Scott brought three motor sleds but only one spare cylinder. After that spare had already been used and one sled had sunk, the second sled and then the third each broke a cylinder and had to be abandoned. One sled could cover seven miles per day and ferry a ton and a half of supplies. Another spare cylinder, even if it had lasted only two days, would have brought One Ton Depot 14 miles farther poleward and saved Scott.

"When expedition zoologist Apsley Cherry-Garrard was finding it hard to learn navigation, Scott commented with indifference, 'Of course there is not one chance in a hundred that he will ever have to consider navigation on our journey.' That one chance materialized at a critical moment: Cherry-Garrard happened to be the only person available to go out with extra supplies and rescue Scott on his return from the Pole. Because Cherry-Garrard couldn't navigate, he didn't proceed beyond One Ton Depot for fear of straying off the route and missing Scott. Instead he sat at the depot for six days while Scott (unbeknownst to Cherry-Garrard) was struggling for his life nearby. Having waited for Scott in vain, Cherry-Garrard headed back to base camp on March 10 — the day before Scott had opium distributed so that his men could choose a nonagonizing death, and one week before Oates committed suicide.

"The supplies that Scott cached in his depots were insufficient for his return journey, even by the most optimistic calculations. From January 20 onward Scott's diary repeatedly notes that he and his companions were hungry, food supplies were low, and they were uncertain if enough food remained to reach the next depot, let alone home base. Yet despite the need to race against time, Scott stopped for half a day on February 8 and again on February 9 to collect geologic specimens. With just one meal left, Scott was lucky to find a depot on February 13 and wrote, 'Yesterday was the worst experience of the trip and gave a horrid feeling of insecurity. Now we are right up, but we must march.' Incredibly, within a few hours of leaving the depot, Scott sent Dr. Wilson to make yet another collection of rocks.

"These examples could be multiplied almost indefinitely. Prudence dictated that Scott plan for a very wide margin of safety. He left none and thereby killed not only himself but four others. . . .

"[Scott's] diaries tell again and again of the complete harmony among his companions, whose diaries and letters written at the same time are criticizing Scott bitterly. Scott drove his men to the point of exhaustion and collapse. The most chilling examples are ones that contributed directly to the men's death.

"On February 28, 1911, Scott ordered the ponies that had laid the first depots to be led back to base camp over newly formed sea ice. When Wilson pointed out that ice conditions were dangerous, Scott blew up and told him that orders were orders. The ice did break up. Three ponies that could have been used to haul more supplies toward the Pole died in that debacle.

"The sole expedition member with any experience of the crucial skill of driving sled dogs single-handedly was Cecil Meares, on whom Scott was depending to bring out supplies for the return journey from the Pole. Yet Scott, who knew nothing of dog sledding and hated it, repeatedly criticized Meares's feeding and driving of the dogs and told him how to do it. Meares eventually became so disgusted that he quit and left by ship. And so it came about that Meares's replacement to bring the dogs to meet Scott was the hapless [unlucky] Cherry-Garrard, who could neither drive dogs nor navigate and could only wait with the dogs at One Ton Depot while Scott was collapsing nearby.

"Scott had promised to include the assistant expedition leader, Teddy Evans, in the polar party. Yet Scott seems to have deliberately worn Evans down by ordering him to discard his skis and slog through the snow. Scott then told the exhausted man to turn back rather than join the race for the Pole. As Evans was about to return, Scott countermanded his previous order that the dogs should meet him at One Ton Depot and instead told Evans to have the dogs meet him 200 miles beyond the depot. But Evans collapsed from scurvy and exhaustion on his return and was unable to report Scott's last instructions. Thus, Cherry-Garrard believed that he was following existing orders by waiting for Scott at One Ton Depot."

Diamond concludes his observations of Scott's ordeal by recalling again the first line from his diary:

" 'The causes of the disaster are not due to faulty organisation, but to misfortune in all risks which had to be undertaken. . . .' The misfortunes that Scott proceeded to enumerate included the loss of the ponies, the shortage of food, and severe weather. Who ordered the ponies to be led over newly formed sea ice? Who had calculated the quantities of food to be cached? Why was it that the dogs did not meet Scott with extra food? Whose task was it to provide an adequate safety margin against severe weather? Scott's last message is a nobly worded evasion of ultimate responsibility. . . .

"But anyone who chronically denies his ultimate responsibility and who tends to seek the fault elsewhere deprives himself of the chance to learn and is condemned to repeat his errors. I would guess that that characteristic was the root of

Scott's tragedy." ("The Price of Human Folly," *Discover* [April 1989], pp. 73–76. Jared Diamond/© 1989 DISCOVER PUBLICATIONS.)

In similar context we have all experienced problems and their consequences because of improper preparation for school work or in organizing a business venture or perhaps by not taking precautions to prevent an illness. If we are careless about risks, we can lose hard-earned money through poor investments or purchase a home or automobile that is not soundly financed. We often end up blaming fate or other people for our own mistakes.

As law is no respecter of persons, so it is with God the Father. He favors nothing which is inconsistent with justice (law), because He has a complete and perfect knowledge of its nature, attributes, functions, and value and submits Himself to it freely. This knowledge can help us better understand Him, His Son Jesus Christ, and many of the events in the history of mankind as the plan of salvation continues to unfold. It helps us to more fully know nature, life, and man's personal responsibility as God's children.

Certainly one can begin to see the need for the principle of mercy to balance the rigid nature of law. We can have more appreciation of the Savior's uncommon role and sacrifice and can be more sure of the need we have for His help in order that the demands of justice, or the strictness of law, can be met.

As we learn of the Father's infinite and absolute respect for and adherence to eternal law, we remember His same respect for the principle of free agency, another of the great governing forces of man's existence. The principle of law and that of free agency work together to enable mankind to reach its highest potential in this way: To expect man to adhere to absolute, binding, unchangeable law would be unfair or unreasonable unless he has his free agency to accept and obey or reject or violate it as it concerns his destiny. Thus, what man chooses, he can in fairness be held accountable for.

As we come back to Adam and Eve once again and contemplate their condition in the garden, we realize that they were purposely placed in a situation where they would have to confront both principles, law and free agency, to accomplish the Lord's plans. They chose to break the one law in order to honor the higher law, which was what the Father desired. It must be appreciated, however, that no matter how much a part of the plan it was that they chose the way they did, *a law was still broken* and natural consequences had to follow. Theirs were twofold: becoming subject to physical death and being cut off from their Father's presence, both of which they willingly accepted. However, the effects of the broken law would then be infinite (everlasting), which was directly opposite of God's plan for His children, so He had to provide for that infinite state to be changed.

This occurred at the time of Jesus' resurrection, which was the bringing together of the body and the spirit, a gift which is free to everyone. Coming back into the presence of their Father once again was earned partly by Adam and Eve through their repentance for breaking the law and their righteous living while on earth, and a part was offered through the mercy of the Savior where they were unable to pay the whole penalty.

In considering Adam and Eve and their circumstances, we can rightfully come to this conclusion: they, far from being the figures of contempt as seen by the world, indeed deserve the greatest degree of gratitude for their efforts on our behalf, and we can have the highest regard and appreciation for them as our first mortal parents.

CHAPTER 4

Live
Before
Dying

Cicero, the great Roman orator, made this observation several years before the birth of Christ:

> No man can be ignorant that he must die, nor be sure that he may not this very day.

Think about it! You and I do not know when our mortal lives will end. It could be many years from now, or "this very day." But one way or another, end they will.

Unfortunately, we have all known persons who died years before they were buried, those who, for all intents and purposes, had given up on life and were "waiting out" the last years. I do not recall ever seeing a child with such an attitude.

The life of the Savior is a perfect example of what we mean by living before dying, and because we are so grateful for His example, we joyously celebrate some of the most glorious events of his life at Christmas and Easter time. However, a true and proper understanding of Christmas and Easter is not just knowing the facts of His birth, death, and resurrection but also having an appreciation of the things that occupied his time and interest in between. Jesus truly *lived* before He died. He loved, understood, and accepted life in all its aspects—the sorrows as well as the joys, the challenges along with the achievements, and he took advantage of the time he had.

While the stories of Christmas and Easter have their inception in the premortal existence, the true spirit of these special days is found in His mortal ministry. Not only did he *live*, but He taught us how to live, also.

Note a sampling of scriptures about the Lord's mortal life. These are not necessarily listed chronologically, but they do contain the spirit of His ministry. He grew, He helped, He suffered, He was compassionate, He became angry, He rejoiced, He smiled, He wept, He understood. He lived! He died! Read and ponder each of the following passages of scripture as you contemplate Christ's mission and sacrifice:

And Jesus increased in wisdom and
stature, and in favour with God and man.
(Luke 2:52)

And it came to pass, that after three
days they found him in the temple,
sitting in the midst of the doctors,
both hearing them, and asking them
questions.
(Luke 2:46)

And it came to pass in those days,
that Jesus came from Nazareth of
Galilee, and was baptized of John in
Jordan.
(Mark 1:9)

And Jesus said unto them, Come ye
after me, and I will make you to become
fishers of men.
(Mark 1:17)

When Jesus saw their faith, he said
unto the sick of the palsy, Son, thy
sins be forgiven thee.

(Mark 2:5)

And it came to pass, that, as Jesus
sat at meat in his [Levi's] house, many
publicans and sinners sat also together
with Jesus and his disciples: for there
were many, and they followed him.

And when the scribes and Pharisees
saw him eat with publicans and sinners,
they said unto his disciples, How is it
that he eateth and drinketh with
publicans and sinners?

When Jesus heard it, he saith unto
them, They that are whole have no need
of the physician, but they that are
sick: I came not to call the righteous,
but sinners to repentance.

(Mark 2:15–17)

And he arose, and rebuked the wind,
and said unto the sea, Peace, be still.
And the wind ceased, and there was a
great calm.

(Mark 4:39)

Then was Jesus led up of the Spirit
into the wilderness to be tempted of the
devil.

And when he had fasted forty days and
forty nights, he was afterward an
hungred.

And when the tempter came to him, he
said, If thou be the Son of God, command
that these stones be made bread.

But he answered and said, It is
written, Man shall not live by bread
alone, but by every word that proceedeth
out of the mouth of God.

(Matthew 4:1–4)

Then said Jesus unto them, I will ask
you one thing; Is it lawful on the
sabbath days to do good, or to do evil?
to save life, or to destroy it?

And looking round about upon them
all, he said unto the man, Stretch forth
thy hand. And he did so: and his hand
was restored whole as the other.

(Luke 6:9–10)

And Jesus went about all the cities
and villages, teaching in their syna-
gogues, and preaching the gospel of
the kingdom, and healing every sickness
and every disease among the people.

But when he saw the multitudes, he
was moved with compassion on them,
because they fainted, and were scattered
abroad, as sheep having no shepherd.

(Matthew 9:35–36)

But I say unto you which hear, Love
your enemies, do good to them which
hate you,

Bless them that curse you, and pray
for them which despitefully use you.

(Luke 6:27–28)

Now when the sun was setting, all
they that had any sick with divers
diseases brought them unto him; and he
laid his hands on every one of them, and
healed them.

(Luke 4:40)

O Jerusalem, Jerusalem, thou that
killest the prophets, and stonest them
which are sent unto thee, how often
would I have gathered thy children
together, even as a hen gathereth her
chickens under her wings, and ye would
not!

(Matthew 23:37)

And he said unto her, Daughter, thy
faith hath made thee whole; go in peace,
and be whole of thy plague.

(Mark 5:34)

And he sighed deeply in his spirit,
and saith, Why doth this generation seek
after a sign? verily I say unto you,
There shall no sign be given unto this
generation.

(Mark 8:12)

But Jesus said, Suffer little children,
and forbid them not, to come unto
me: for of such is the kingdom of
heaven.

And he laid his hands on them, and
departed thence.

(Matthew 19:14–15)

And the Jews' passover was at hand,
and Jesus went up to Jerusalem,

And found in the temple those that
sold oxen and sheep and doves, and the
changers of money sitting:

And when he had made a scourge of
small cords, he drove them all out of
the temple, and the sheep, and the oxen;
and poured out the changers' money, and
overthrew the tables;

And said unto them that sold doves,
Take these things hence; make not my
Father's house an house of merchandise.
(John 2:13–16)

And they spit upon him, and took the
reed, and smote him on the head.
(Matthew 27:30)

When Jesus therefore saw his mother,
and the disciple standing by, whom he
loved, he saith unto his mother, Woman,
behold thy son!
Then saith he to the disciple, Behold
thy mother! And from that hour that
disciple took her unto his own home.
(John 19:26–27)

And about the ninth hour Jesus cried
with a loud voice, saying, Eli, Eli, lama
sabachthani? that is to say, My God, my
God, why hast thou forsaken me?
(Matthew 27:46)

Jesus, when he had cried again with a
loud voice, yielded up the ghost.
(Matthew 27:50)

Jesus saith unto her, Woman, why
weepest thou? whom seekest thou? She,
supposing him to be the gardener, saith
unto him, Sir, if thou have borne him
hence, tell me where thou hast laid him,
and I will take him away.
Jesus saith unto her, Mary. She
turned herself, and saith unto him,
Rabboni; which is to say, Master.

> Jesus saith unto her, Touch me not;
> for I am not yet ascended to my Father:
> but go to my brethren, and say unto
> them, I ascend unto my Father, and your
> Father; and to my God, and your God.
> Mary Magdalene came and told the
> disciples that she had seen the Lord,
> and that he had spoken these things unto
> her.
> (John 20:15–18)

In the four Gospels of the New Testament, there are few references to the actual events of Jesus' life. But they are representative. They demonstrate the Savior's love of life and His understanding of its many challenges. While Christ lived, He lived to the fullest. Having lived and loved life, His death and resurrection are even more remarkable. The giving of His life was truly a sacrifice!

In the spirit of those scriptures, think about this true life experience of a father and his daughter:

"The hospital was unusually quiet that bleak January evening; quiet and still like the air before a storm. I glanced at the clock in the nurse's station. It was nine o'clock. I threw a stethoscope around my neck and headed for room 712.

"As I entered the room, Mr. Mills looked up eagerly, but dropped his eyes when he saw it was only me, his nurse. I pressed the stethoscope to his chest and listened. Strong, slow, even beating. There seemed little indication he had suffered a slight heart attack a few hours earlier.

"He looked up, tears filling his eyes. I touched his hand, waiting. 'Would you call my daughter?' he asked at last. 'You see, I live alone and she is the only family I have.' His respiration suddenly speeded up.

"I increased his oxygen supply. 'Of course, I'll call her,' I said.

"He gripped the sheets and pulled himself forward, his face tense with urgency. 'Will you call her right away—as soon as you can?'

"He was breathing fast, too fast. 'I'll call her the very first thing,' I said patting his shoulder. 'Now you get some rest.'

"He closed his eyes. Reluctant to leave, I moved through the shadowy silence to the window. The panes were cold. Below, a foggy mist moved through the hospital parking lot. Snow clouds quilted the night sky.

" 'Nurse,' he called, 'could you get me a pencil and paper?'

"I dug a scrap of yellow paper and pen from my pocket and set them on the bedside table. 'Thank you,' he said. I smiled at him and left.

"Mr. Mills's daughter was listed on his chart as the next of kin. I got her number from information.

" 'Miss Janie Mills, this is Sue Kidd, a nurse at the hospital. I'm calling about your father. He was admitted tonight with a heart attack and . . .'

" 'No!' she screamed into the phone, startling me. 'He's not dying is he?' It was more of a plea than a question.

" 'His condition is stable at the moment,' I said, trying to sound convincing.

" 'You must not let him die!' she said. Her voice was so compelling that my hand trembled on the phone.

" 'He's getting the very best care.'

" 'But you don't understand,' she pleaded. 'Dad and I had a terrible argument almost a year ago. I . . . I haven't seen him since. All these months I've wanted to go to him for forgiveness. The last thing I said to him was, "I hate you." '

"Her voice cracked and I heard her heave great agonizing sobs. I listened, tears burning my eyes. A father and a daughter, so lost to each other. Then I was thinking of my own father, many miles away. It had been so long since I said, 'I love you.'

"As Janie struggled to control her tears, I breathed a prayer: 'Please God, let this daughter find forgiveness.'

" 'I'm coming now! I'll be there in thirty minutes,' she said and hung up.

"I tried to busy myself with a stack of charts on the desk,

but I couldn't concentrate. Room 712. I felt I had to get back to 712! I hurried down the hall nearly in a run.

"Mr. Mills lay unmoving. I reached for his pulse. There was none.

" 'Code 99. Room 712. Code 99. Room 712.' The alert was sounded through the hospital seconds after the switchboard was notified.

"Mr. Mills had had a cardiac arrest. I leveled the bed and bent over his mouth, breathing air into his lungs. I positioned my hands over his chest and compressed. One, two, three. At fifteen, I moved back to his mouth and breathed as deeply as I could. Where was help? Again I compressed and breathed. Compressed and breathed.

" 'Oh, God,' I prayed, 'his daughter is coming. Don't let it end this way.'

"The door burst open. Doctors and nurses pushed emergency equipment into the room. A doctor took over the manual compression of the heart. A tube was inserted through the patient's mouth as an airway. Nurses plunged syringes of medicine into the intravenous tubing.

"I watched the heart monitor. Nothing. Not a beat. 'Stand back!' cried a doctor. I handed him the paddles for the electric shock to the heart. He placed them on Mr. Mills's chest. Over and over we tried, but nothing. No response.

"A nurse turned off the oxygen. The gurgling stopped. One by one they left, grim and silent. I stood by his bed, stunned. Wind rattled the window, pelting the panes with snow. How could I face his daughter?

"When I left the room I saw her. A doctor who had been inside 712 only moments before stood talking to her, gripping her elbow. Then he moved on, leaving Janie slumped against the wall. Such pathetic hurt in her face. Such wounded eyes.

"I took her hand and led her into the nurses' lounge. We sat, neither of us saying a word. She stared straight ahead, glass-faced, breakable-looking.

" 'Janie, I'm sorry,' I said. It was pitifully inadequate.

" 'I never hated him, you know. I loved him,' she said. She whirled toward me. 'I want to see him.'

"My first thought was, why put yourself through more pain? But I got up and wrapped my arm around her. We walked slowly down the corridor to 712. She pushed open the door, went to the bed, and buried her face in the sheets.

"I tried not to look at this sad good-bye. I backed into the bedtable and as I did, my hand fell upon a scrap of yellow paper. I picked it up. It read:

" 'My dearest Janie, I forgive you. I pray you will also forgive me. I know that you love me. I love you, too. Daddy.'

"The note was shaking in my hands as I thrust it toward Janie. She read it once. Then twice. Peace began to glisten in her eyes. She hugged the scrap of paper to her breast.

" 'Thank you God,' I whispered, looking up at the window. A few crystal stars blinked through the blackness. A snowflake hit the window and melted away, gone forever. 'Thank you, God, that relationships, sometimes fragile as snowflakes, can be mended together again . . . but there is not a moment to spare.'

"I tiptoed from the room and hurried to the telephone. I would call my father. I would say, 'I love you.' " (From Sue Monk Kidd, "Don't Let It End This Way," *Guideposts*, June 1979. Excerpted with permission from Guideposts Magazine. Copyright © 1979 by Guideposts Associates, Inc., Carmel, NY 10512.)

What a lesson! Perhaps such accounts can assist us all to live life a little more fully.

Those who may be somewhat familiar with the customs of the Middle East will know that a simple oil lamp is used to light many homes. It is a small clay vessel with the front end pinched together to form an opening. A piece of flax, serving as the wick, is inserted through the small hole until part of it is submerged in the oil. When the flax is saturated, it can be lighted. It will then burn with a soft, warm glow. But when the oil in the lamp is consumed, the flax will dry out. When ignited again, it gives off an acrid, dirty smoke, making the vessel offensive and useless. Now, one might think that the only thing to do would be to crush and discard the wick. But that would accomplish nothing. If you refill the lamp with oil, the wick can burn as brightly as before.

My point is simple. We need to fill our lives to the fullest, to:

study and learn	develop our talents
experience struggle	solve problems
enjoy the earth's beauty	serve others
overcome weaknesses	achieve success
love and teach our families	make friends
feel sorrow	accept trials
form positive attitudes	appreciate blessings
pray	set goals
engage actively in good works	develop Christlike virtues

We need and will be called upon to do these things over and over again. We need to "burn brightly" our whole lives. It just doesn't make any sense to sit in mortality and "give off smoke"—especially when we have a choice to do otherwise! We need to take advantage of our lives. Remember what Cicero said about the unpredictability of life? We will all die, but since we don't know when that will be, let's enjoy our lives to the fullest, let's make of them all that our Father in Heaven intended for us. Let's remember the scripture, "Man is that he might have joy," a joy that comes not only from pleasant experiences but also from "subduing the earth" and mastering ourselves. This the Savior so aptly taught us to do through His example of service, love, understanding, rejoicing, compassion, suffering, and sacrifice.

There is no doubt that Christ loved life. He enjoyed people. He loved this mortal existence and what it had to offer. I find no indication that He wanted to terminate life prematurely, but His mission was to become the Redeemer of the world. He loved mankind as He loved His Father, and even though His life on earth had meaning and purpose He willingly laid it down in order that mankind might be resurrected and once again regain God's presence!

CHAPTER 5

No Greater Gift

S cores of times as I have attended funerals
within my own faith and elsewhere,
speakers have phrased again the question of the ages as recorded in Job:

If a man die, shall he live again?
(Job 14:14.)

This question has been pondered, wondered about, and
asked many hundreds of times through all ages gone by and
will be asked continually as long as man lives on the earth,
not merely as a scientific or information-seeking question but
more often as an emotional one in times of crisis, great personal loss, grief, or sometimes tragedy or fear; at the passing
of loved ones, trusted friends, or respected associates; or perhaps at a time of our own pending death. Strangely enough,
many of us, in less desperate, more normal times, know in
fact and readily accept the answer as part of our mortal experience—until we are faced with the actual reality of passing
into an unknown sphere, of separation. Then we often become frantic for assurance that what we "know" will actually
occur. And those who have yet to come to this knowledge are
possibly more frantic.

After all, the only experiences we can recall are right here,
and at best we can't imagine improving on the situation. We

aren't always full of joy though, and yet even at less than best, earth life is all we know, and that knowledge carries with it great security as opposed to changing our bodily status, our surroundings and activities, and bringing to an end the many beauties and experiences we enjoy and love.

And then there are the relationships we have developed, those choice people we love and cherish and without whom no life anywhere would be the same.

Perhaps the real questions we're asking in more descriptive terms would be:

"If I die where will I be?"

"Will I still be me?"

"Will I have the chance of improving myself?"

"Will I continue to enjoy the things I have learned and have excelled in?"

"Can I learn more of the things I yearn to know?"

"Will I be reunited with those I love? Heaven could not be heaven without them!"

Oh yes, I'm sure the question of a life after death will continue to be asked.

Not long ago I sat on the stand with a colleague during the funeral services for a lovely young woman who had been brutally murdered. Her husband and daughters sat before us. The chapel was filled to overflowing. Family, friends, and neighbors were gathered together to pay tribute to a wonderful young mother. In addition, there were men and women who had never known or met this family. A thoughtful, sensitive Catholic priest from a nearby parish sat next to me. We were all there: family, friends, neighbors, acquaintances, strangers, the press, the concerned. All waited. I could sense deep down the question many wanted to hear answered one more time: "If a young mother die, shall she live again?" Each speaker in turn answered that question in positive terms and with a strong personal witness. In word and music the answer was, *"Yes!"* When we die, we all shall surely live again.

I have long admired little children and have appreciated so much their wonderful talent of putting things in perspective. The story is told of a little boy who came home from Sunday School one day and was asked by his mother what he had learned. He said, "My teacher told us that I used to be dust and I would return to dust once more. Is that true, Mommy?"

"Yes," the mother replied. "A scripture tells us so: 'For dust thou art, and unto dust shalt thou return' " (Genesis 3:19).

The little boy was amazed at this! The next morning, he was scurrying around getting ready for school, looking for his shoes. He looked under his bed. Lo and behold, there he saw balls of dust. He ran to his mother and said, "Oh, Mommy, somebody's under my bed, and I can't tell whether they're coming or going."

Children make such practical observations. The boy's comment was in one sense accurate. Many are still coming and we are all going. We are all in the process of aging and we will all eventually die, a fact that is often difficult to accept, especially when we are in our youth or in the prime of life.

A ten-year-old girl recorded in her personal journal these tender events in her young life:

"April 18

"Mom gave me this journal and told me to write about some of the things that happen to me. I really like reading journals of other people, but I don't know if I'll ever have anything very interesting to write about.

"May 21

"Mom still hadn't baked bread when I got home from school today, and she promised. She was in her bedroom, sleeping again. By the looks of the house, she must have been in bed all day. I'm glad I did the breakfast dishes before school, or they would have still been sitting there.

"I played at Susan's until Dad came home; then we fixed dinner. Mom wasn't hungry and Dad didn't eat very much. He has sure been a grouch lately.

"May 22

"Dad came in and talked to me last night. He told me that Mom is really sick and that I'll have to help around the house a lot more. Dad often laughs and jokes, but I've never seen him cry before.

"It's night now. I worked hard all day and I'm tired.

"May 24

"School is out Wednesday and I'm glad. It's kind of hard to go to school and take care of a house and everything. I'm glad I'm only ten and won't get married for a lot of years. There isn't much time to play when you have work to do. Susan says I'm getting stuck-up because I don't play with her anymore. But her mother isn't sick.

"Dad let me fix pancakes this morning all by myself. They tasted really good, but Dad must not have been hungry because he only ate one. . . .

"May 30

"We all went to Sunday School today. Mom looked so pretty in her blue dress. She made it last month, but she hasn't worn it before. She slept on Dad's shoulder through part of the opening exercise, but no one seemed to care. We went for a short walk after sacrament meeting and talked about our plans for tomorrow. . . .

"June 10

"It doesn't seem fair—Mom sleeps and does nothing and hates it; I do her work and I hate that. Ten years old isn't old enough to be a mother. And even if I'm not anybody's mother, I have to do everything anyway. I guess I'll just have to try harder.

"Mom showed me how to iron today. Don't tell me no one irons anymore, because we do. My dad has to wear cotton shirts so his arms don't get rashy.

"Mom got tired and had to go back to bed, so I ironed the last shirt alone. When Dad got home, he said I was really growing up; and he just stood there and looked at his shirt for a long time.

"P.S. When I went in for a drink just now, Dad was putting away the ironing board. His shirt looked better. How did he get those wrinkles out?

"June 23

"I have really been busy, but it's been fun. Dad and I picked twenty pounds of strawberries on Saturday. We washed and stemmed six pounds, cut them in half, and put them into the dryer. The next six pounds we made into strawberry jam. That was fun and we both laughed a lot. Maybe because he is so big and his voice is so deep, I used to be kind of scared of him. But I'm not anymore. Either I'm growing up or I understand him better.

"Anyway, we also made strawberry shortcake for dinner and put the rest of the berries into the freezer. They'll taste good next winter.

"Mom came out to the kitchen and watched for a while, but she couldn't help. I picked out the biggest, reddest berry I could find and gave it to her. Strawberries have always been her favorite fruit. . . .

"July 23

"Dad ate three of my pancakes this morning. It's the first time he has been that hungry. Sister Hunt came over and we baked bread. *Umm-m-m!* I can still smell and taste it. I'm going to like staying home and baking bread when I'm a mother. I know my kids will like it too. I don't mind dusting the furniture and making it shiny, but I hate to do the bathroom. I'm glad we don't have four boys around here like Susan does. Boys make a horrible mess in the bathroom sink.

"Dad and I take turns reading the Book of Mormon to Mom at night. She likes to hear it. I don't really understand all of it, but it makes me feel good.

"Dad talks to me a lot now. He said tonight that Mom will soon be going away. His voice sounded funny and he hugged me. I guess he means she is going to die. I can't make myself believe it. I think that's because I don't want to.

"August 8

"When I woke up this morning Mom and Dad were gone, and Sister Hunt was fixing my breakfast. She said that Mom got sick in the night and Dad took her to the hospital. I'm going to stay with Sister Hunt for a while.

"August 12

"I heard Dad come in tonight and talk with Brother and Sister Hunt. I was hoping he would come and talk to me, but he didn't. Something wouldn't let me get up and go see him.

"August 13

"Sister Hunt was sitting in my room when I woke up this morning. She sat on my bed and just held me in her arms for a few minutes, and I knew what she was going to say. At last she told me that Mom has gone back to our Heavenly Father. I just nodded. When she went back into the kitchen, I put my head under the covers and cried.

"August 17

"I don't remember much about the funeral. Mom looked peaceful in her white dress. I kept thinking it was all a dream and I would wake up and we would be a happy family again. I even pinched myself to be sure I was awake. Everyone is gone now but Dad and me. It's sure quiet.

"September 10

"I can hardly wait to tell Dad about my dream. I saw Mom and she was smiling and pretty again. I was sitting on her lap and I could smell the flowers in her hair. She told me to be happy and that we would all be together again someday, and it would be better than ever. I'm almost happy.

"SAME DAY. Guess what! Dad dreamed about Mom too. He said tomorrow we'll go on a picnic. Just the two of us!" (Rae Merritt, "My Journal," *Friend*, May 1979, pp. 13–16.)

The reality of death is hard to accept, but to more understandably face it we must bring to mind once again the knowledge that life here on earth, as wonderful, joyous, and fulfilling as it is and was intended to be, was never meant to be an end in and of itself. Rather, it is a brief, extremely purposeful period, a tiny segment of time which is a part of a much larger pattern or scheme of things and was prepared long, long ago for our complete and eternal existence. It is natural, having forgotten the wholeness of the plan we once knew and understood so well in our premortal life, to become very concerned at the thought of leaving the only experiences that are familiar to us—our earthly surroundings and the relationships we have come to love and value and with which we have security. Therefore a parting from earth life can seem like a tragedy. In actual fact it is just one more step in our intended progress, which, if properly understood, can bring great comfort, tremendous appreciation, and a glorious promise for the future.

As all men die, so shall they live through God's greatest gift, the atonement of Jesus Christ.

President John Taylor taught:

> In some mysterious, incomprehensible way, Jesus assumed the responsibility which naturally would have devolved upon Adam; but which could only be accomplished through the mediation of Himself, and by taking upon Himself their sorrows, assuming their responsibilities and bearing their transgressions or sins. . . . He bore the weight of the sins of the whole world; not only of Adam, but of his posterity; and in doing that, opened the kingdom of heaven, not only to all believers and all who obeyed the law of God, but to more than one-half of the human family who die before they come to years of maturity, as well as to the heathen, who, having died without law, will, through His mediation, be resurrected without law, and be judged without law, and thus participate, according to their capacity, works and worth, in the blessings of His atonement. (*The Mediation and Atonement* [Salt Lake City: Deseret News Co., 1882], pp. 148–49.)

Three Important Keys

To fully appreciate the Atonement, I have found it helpful to carefully consider and have understanding of three very important factors which are an integral part of that great event and without which the event would not have occurred at all.

Love

Christ lived, taught, and died because of His great love, understanding, and compassion for mankind. His entire life and mission were devoted to teaching and encouraging, guiding and preparing, and physically and spiritually making it possible for man to receive the great gift of the resurrection and the opportunity to gain, with the Savior's help, eternal life for himself through repentance, and to once again live in and enjoy the presence of his Heavenly Father.

Nephi records:

> For behold, my beloved brethren, I say unto you that the Lord God worketh not in darkness.
>
> He doeth not anything save it be for the benefit of the world; for he loveth the world, even that he layeth down his own life that he may draw all men unto him. Wherefore, he commandeth none that they shall not partake of his salvation. (2 Nephi 26:23–24.)

And how great must be the love of our Heavenly Father for us that He would send His only Begotten Son to suffer so terribly and die for the rest of His children.

> For God so loved the world, that he gave his only begotten Son, that whosoever believeth in him should not perish, but have everlasting life (John 3:16).

And further:

> He that loveth not knoweth not God; for God is love.
>
> In this was manifested the love of God toward us, because that God sent his only begotten Son into the world, that we might live through him.
>
> Herein is love, not that we loved God, but that he loved us, and sent his Son to be the propitiation [the atoning sacrifice] for our sins.
>
> Beloved, if God so loved us, we ought also to love one another. (1 John 4:8–11.)

Of course, understanding the type and depth of the love that our Heavenly Father and His Son have for man, love sufficient to enable them to make such tremendous, unbelievable sacrifices, is incomprehensible to us. It is far beyond our capacity to grasp at this point in our existence. However, in our own realm of understanding and in comparatively insignificant ways, we may be able to relate to those feelings. We have all experienced deep compassion and perhaps have sacrificed for someone at some time or another, and we have seen and heard of these events in the lives of others.

My own brother David tells of an experience involving the two of us as youngsters that to this day he says causes the greatest feelings of compassion.

"When I was about nine years old and Paul was a couple of years older, I found one day in our basement a long, round metal curtain rod, the kind that was commonly used in those days. It looked just like a wooden dowel only it was solid brass, about three and a half feet long and one-quarter inch in circumference and was perfectly straight with no curved ends the way most curtain rods are made today. Though I was certainly familiar with curtain rods, when I saw that pole it looked nothing like a curtain rod to me. The only thing that registered in my mind was 'spear!'

"At that time Tarzan movies were very popular, and we went to the movie theatre every time one of his pictures came to town. Almost every one I ever saw had lots of natives

throwing long spears at Tarzan as he swung back and forth
from tree to tree, and I daydreamed constantly about myself
throwing one of those spears and *hitting* the target, which the
natives never seemed to do. Now as I picked up that rod, I
thought my dreams had surely come true. I got upstairs and
outside with it and tried a few trial heaves. It was quite an effort, for a while, to throw it at all because of its length and
weight, but I finally managed to get it to stick into the ground,
and the results were amazing. The rod was so long that when
it went down into the ground it made a twanging noise and
then the top vibrated back and forth for a long time before it
stopped still. At the time, it was the most exciting thing I'd
ever seen!

"It happened to be summertime—no school—so I had
ample time to practice my new sport, and practice I did, day
in and day out—I never got tired of throwing that 'spear.'
Paul was quite interested in it, too, and we decided, finally,
that it would stick into more things if it had a point on it. We
used the sidewalk for that purpose, scraping that rod back
and forth, back and forth, till it lost its blunt end, which
seemed to take forever. But then the enjoyment of the throwing was greater than ever. I became so good at pitching my
spear that I seldom missed anything I tried to hit—and always
the 'twang' and the vibrating! I tried throwing it by my foot
to see how close I could get without hitting myself, and I was
really good. In fact I thought I was almost perfect and did a
lot of bragging!

"One afternoon some of my mother's friends walked by
while I was throwing and I felt motivated, as boys often are,
to prove my great abilities, so I threw the spear a few places
and they seemed impressed. Then I saw Paul coming around
the house and I shouted to him to come try an experiment
with me. He willingly obliged because he was quite pleased at
my success himself, being, even then, a sportsman in his own
right. I told him to stick out his foot to see how close I could
throw the rod to it, and, knowing my skill, he planted his foot
right out there. I reared back and let that rod fly, and never in

my whole experience have I been as shocked as I was in that instant. Instead of pointing into the dirt where I'd aimed it, it missed that goal, it even missed Paul's foot, and stuck, to my great horror, into his leg above the ankle. Well, you can imagine the scene—blood, stress calls, neighbors and Mom running, our dog barking—and the look on Paul's face! . . . It's the worst experience I can ever remember. I looked at Paul in his agony and I remember actually feeling the intense pain myself—my leg hurt, my foot hurt, in fact I hurt all over. I cried, and Paul cried and screamed, and I remember someone coming who knew the right thing to do and did it. Finally things calmed down, the doctor was called, and Paul began to get some relief; and luckily, though the wound was extremely painful, there was no terrible permanent damage. The lasting effect was in me—not guilt, because I knew it had been an accident, but pure anguish for my brother as I realized how he was hurting. The real pain of my thoughts and feelings has subsided now but certainly not the memory of the compassion I had that day!"

Consider this incident of sacrifice for another:

"It is related of Lord Byron that when he was a lad attending school, a companion of his fell under the displeasure of an overbearing bully, who unmercifully beat him. Byron happened to be present, but knowing the uselessness of undertaking a fight with the bully, he stepped up to him and asked him how much longer he intended to beat his friend.

" 'What's that to you?' gruffly demanded the bully.

" 'Because,' replied young Byron, the tears standing in his eyes, 'I will take the rest of the beating if you will let him go.' " (As recounted in B. H. Roberts, *The Gospel and Man's Relationship to Deity* [Salt Lake City: Deseret Book Co., 1965], p. 15.)

Think about this poignant example of a mother's love:

"A wonderful little infant blessed the life of this woman on the day she became a mother. He was a darling baby, but he had one problem—he was born without ears. Tests proved later that his hearing was perfect, but the child simply had no outer ears. And in his early years, though his mother tried so hard, he never let himself be totally consoled as older children and his own peers thoughtlessly teased him and called him names.

"The boy began to develop talents as he grew up and, had it not been for his missing outer ears, might have been considered strikingly handsome. A doctor decided that ears could be grafted on, but finding a suitable donor would be difficult. Then one day the father told him that such a donor had been found. This donor requested only that the young man never learn who gave him his ears.

"The operation was a success. The boy's talents flourished under his newfound confidence. His schooling and career seemed to consist of nothing but success after success. And never would his parents betray the donor's secret.

"At last the day came when the son stood alongside his father and wept over his mother's casket. As they stood there, the father slowly stretched forth his hand and raised his dear wife's hair—she had no outer ears. She had given her ears to lessen her son's pain with no thought of how she might be inconvenienced herself." (As related in Paul H. Dunn, *Seek the Happy Life* [Salt Lake City: Bookcraft, 1985], p. 105.)

Without the compassion, love, and empathy shown through such touching experiences as these, mankind would not make much progress in human relationships. And through these same experiences we can perhaps grasp an infinitesimal portion of the depth of love, compassion, and sacrifice felt and suffered by our Savior.

> He that loveth not knoweth not God. . . . If God so loved us, we ought also to love one another.

The divine and unconditional love that our Father and His Son have for us is, in my mind, one of the three key factors that permit us to more fully understand the Atonement. The other two factors, eternal law and free agency, have been presented in previous chapters for the benefit of the subjects under discussion there, but it is my intent to refer back to them from time to time, and I do so now, as they shed light on what I am attempting to explain here.

Eternal Law

The vital key of eternal law greatly affects our appreciation of Jesus' sacrifice for us. The necessity for the Atonement, a law in itself, was brought about by the breaking of another law, by Adam, thus causing the Fall. Neither of these two events can be fully, effectively understood without knowledge of the other or without being seen as part of the whole plan of salvation. The two events go together hand in hand as night follows day.

> For since by man came death, by man came also the resurrection of the dead.
> For as in Adam all die, even so in Christ shall all be made alive. (1 Corinthians 15:21–22.)

Or in other words, the violation of one law, necessary as that violation was, was canceled out by the application of another law.

We know that the plan for both events was presented in the premortal life, that it was thoroughly understood by us, both as to its need and its format, and was joyously and wholeheartedly accepted by us. Both acts working together were necessary to make possible the attainment of ultimate goals while at the same time keeping strict adherence to the demands or requirements of the law. The responsibility for carrying out both acts, the breaking of a law in the Garden of Eden and the resulting payment of the penalty of that law, or the righting of that wrong, was willingly accepted by Adam and Jesus Christ, the initiators of the acts.

The attempt has been made to show throughout this account of the great and divine plan that the effects of eternal law are felt in every phase of existence.

Eternal law, or truth, is one of the choicest and most valuable assets and blessings in our lives. True, it is harsh and inflexible by nature in its demands of perfect adherence to its conditions. At the same time, however, it becomes a reliable constant, a dependable standard, one that can always be counted on. It is a security, indeed a promise of consistency by which we can gauge moral and scientific behavior, obtain certain positive results in our various areas of achievement, and reach desirable personal goals. All this is possible if we are careful to conform to laws' precepts.

As has been said, God Himself submits to these laws. He is, without exception, a God of law and without that truth He would cease to be God:

> Behold mine house is a house of order, saith the Lord God, and not a house of confusion (D&C 132:8).

Free Agency

Another vital key to the Atonement is the principle of free agency, also an extremely important blessing to us as a governing factor in our lives. Working together with and in respect for law, it gives us the privilege, in fact the responsibility, the duty, within certain limits and based on various circumstances, of designing for ourselves almost any kind of life situation, mind set, and attitude that we desire.

> For behold, it is not meet that I should command in all things; for he that is compelled in all things, the same is a slothful and not a wise servant; wherefore he receiveth no reward.
>
> Verily I say, men should be anxiously engaged in a good cause, and do many things of their own free will, and bring to pass much righteousness;
>
> For the power is in them, wherein they are agents unto themselves. And inasmuch as men do good they shall in nowise lose their reward.
>
> But he that doeth not anything until he is commanded, and receiveth a commandment with doubtful heart, and keepeth it with slothfulness, the same is damned [limited in his progress]. (D&C 58:26–29.)

Not only did free agency play its roll in the Council of Heaven and the Garden of Eden, but it is central in our mortal successes and failures, progress and retrogression, joys and miseries. It is an imperative key to repentance and to our ultimate destiny in the postmortal world. We must *choose* to meet the conditions necessary for our eternal life.

It is a principle which we must assume is as eternal as our intelligence and is honored implicitly by Deity in every instance. Man is meant to be free. He is meant to choose for himself, not in the sense of simply having his own way, of doing just as he pleases at all times regardless of others needs and rights or of eternal or man-made law, but rather as he functions within the established conditions, limits, and laws of his universe and society.

Taking into account the validity of Dr. Lowell Bennion's statement, "Man's freedom is relative, not absolute," still he is meant to be "a free agent unto himself."

Scripture testifies to this truth.

Therefore, cheer up your hearts, and remember that ye are free to act for yourselves—to choose the way of everlasting death or the way of eternal life (2 Nephi 10:23).

And now remember, remember, my brethren, that whosoever perisheth, perisheth unto himself; and whosoever doeth iniquity, doeth it unto himself; for behold, ye are free; ye are permitted to act for yourselves; for behold, God hath given unto you a knowledge and he hath made you free (Helaman 14:30).

Abide ye in the liberty wherewith ye are made free; entangle not yourselves in sin, but let your hands be clean, until the Lord comes (D&C 88:86).

I, the Lord God, make you free, therefore ye are free indeed; and the law also maketh you free (D&C 98:8).

Keep in mind, however, that the only true freedom is the freedom to live within the law.

The Atonement

The fall of Adam, according to the foreordained plan, was for the purpose of establishing an earth life where men could acquire necessary mortal bodies and more effectively prepare for eternity. It brought death into existence, death of two kinds. One death was temporal or physical death—the separation, at some point in his life, of man's body from his spirit. This would have terrifying and devastating consequences for us because of the importance of our physical bodies as tools to enable us to live in eternity as well as in mortality.

The other death was spiritual death—man's separation from the presence of his Heavenly Father because of his condition of unworthiness. Because the Father can tolerate "no unclean thing" in the kingdom of heaven, and because any violation of law assumes unworthiness or uncleanliness in light of the demand for obedience and payment, Adam and Eve were not allowed to remain with their Father because of their "unworthiness." We do not believe, of course, that they actually were unclean or unworthy, but in performing that act of violation of law necessary for man's eventual redemption, they took the responsibility and the accompanying sacrifice unto themselves.

As the generations of Adam and Eve's posterity came to earth and lived their lives, they, through ignorance, lack of understanding, and through their subjectivity to the conditions of opposition, often chose to follow unrighteous paths rather than those of obedience to law. They in turn, then, also alienated or separated themselves from the Father. Continually through the ages to our times, all men everywhere, for these same reasons, have committed wrongdoings, have made unfortunate mistakes, have sinned, and have therefore become personally unworthy. To this extent we too are separated from our Father both spiritually and physically, just as were our first mortal parents.

The Atonement, then—the supreme sacrifice of Jesus Christ—was provided to lend mercy, to heal these wounds and overcome these potentially tragic conditions. Christ, in perfect knowledge and understanding of our needs and of the consequences to Himself, personally took the act upon Himself as a voluntary sacrifice for mankind because of his love for us, this love, again, being one of the three vital keys to our appreciation of the Atonement.

Jesus' sacrifice had a twofold purpose, just as the violation of the law itself had had a twofold consequence. One aspect of His atonement would join together once again the bodies and the spirits of all mankind. The other aspect would make it possible for men to be reconciled with their Heavenly Father, to once again gain His presence, and to be forgiven for their sins through repentance. To bring this about Christ died physically, after having taken unto and upon Himself the whole responsibility for mankind's violation of law. He Himself willingly and mercifully suffered any further consequences or penalties which would come to us in addition to the unavoidable natural consequences we had already experienced for breaking eternal law.

Temporal Death

The one separation, temporal or physical death, while caused by Adam's transgression, was inherited as a legacy by his posterity, although they, themselves, had had nothing to do with Adam's choice. Therefore, in mercy and fairness, they were not held accountable for the act. A restoring to or redeeming of the original condition of the body and spirit was needed to free them from the effects of the broken law, however, and that redemption was the Resurrection.

Jesus hung on the cross in indescribable agony that would be impossible for us to identify with.

And then after death had finally, mercifully come, He was placed in a tomb from which he quietly but triumphantly rose three days later, very much alive physically. In doing so he proclaimed to the world and all generations of time the reality and glory of the principle of atonement. He also taught by vivid example that His, the first, resurrection would be the pattern and the blessing for the whole of mankind. It would be their saving from the everlasting death in which their mortal bodies would turn to dust in their graves and their eternal spirits would exist forever in misery. This temporal death of all men is replaced by immortality or everlasting life, but not necessarily exaltation. At that time our bodies will be purified, perfected, and fitted for a never-ending existence, and rejoined with our spirits, making it possible for us to live forever.

This blessing is a gift through the grace of God and is absolutely free and unconditional to *all* men, a gift that we don't earn for ourselves. Regardless of our obedience or disobedience, our faith or lack of it, irrespective of any action on our part, we will all gain resurrection, and physical death will come to an everlasting end. And if even one soul remained unsaved in this way, Christ would not win the victory over death, which we know, of course, that He did.

Amulek shared this great truth when he taught:

> Now, there is a death which is called a temporal death; and the death of Christ shall loose the bands of this temporal death, that all shall be raised from this temporal death.
>
> The spirit and the body shall be reunited again in its perfect form; both limb and joint shall be restored to its proper frame, even as we now are at this time; and we shall be brought to stand before God, knowing even as we know now, and have a bright recollection of all our guilt.
>
> Now, this restoration shall come to all, both old and young, both bond and free, both male and female, both the wicked and the righteous; and even there shall not so much as a hair of their heads be lost; but every thing shall be restored to its perfect frame, as it is now, or in the body, and shall be brought and be arraigned before the bar of Christ the Son, and God the Father, and the Holy Spirit, which is one Eternal God, to be judged according to their works, whether they be good or whether they be evil.
>
> Now, behold, I have spoken unto you concerning the death of the mortal body, and also concerning the resurrec-

tion of the mortal body. I say unto you that this mortal body is raised to an immortal body, that is from death, even from the first death unto life, that they can die no more; their spirits uniting with their bodies, never to be divided; thus the whole becoming spiritual and immortal, that they can no more see corruption. (Alma 11:42–45.)

Note these related teachings, first from Moroni and then from Paul:

Behold, he created Adam, and by Adam came the fall of man. And because of the fall of man came Jesus Christ, even the Father and the Son; and because of Jesus Christ came the redemption of man.

. . . Yea, this is wherein all men are redeemed, because the death of Christ bringeth to pass the resurrection, which bringeth to pass a redemption from an endless sleep, from which sleep all men shall be awakened by the power of God when the trump shall sound; and they shall come forth, both small and great, and all shall stand before his bar, being redeemed and loosed from this eternal band of death, which death is a temporal death. (Mormon 9:12–13.)

Then cometh the end, when he shall have delivered up the kingdom to God, even the Father; when he shall have put down all rule and all authority and power.

For he must reign, till he hath put all enemies under his feet.

The last enemy that shall be destroyed is death. (1 Corinthians 15:24–26.)

Spiritual Death

The words of a favorite hymn teach a great lesson about our Redeemer, about His Father—our Father—and about a very important principle or law. As we now consider the second purpose of the Atonement, these words give us much food for thought:

Know this, that every soul is free
To choose his life and what he'll be;
For this eternal truth is given:
That God will force no man to heaven [celestial kingdom].

He'll call, persuade, direct a-right,
And bless with wisdom, love, and light,
In nameless ways be good and kind,
But never force the human mind. . . .

May we no more our powers abuse,
But ways of truth and goodness choose;
Our God is pleased when we improve
His grace [gift] and seek his perfect love.
("Know This, That Every Soul Is Free," *Hymns*, no. 240.)

In the New Testament, Christ gives us, through the book of Revelation, a promise and a challenge that echo the message of this beautiful hymn:

> Behold, I stand at the door, and knock: if any man hear my voice, and open the door, I will come in to him, and will sup with him, and he with me.
> To him that overcometh will I grant to sit with me in my throne, even as I also overcame, and am set down with my Father in his throne. (Revelation 3:20–21.)

With this compassionate plea from Him whose whole being, mind, and work were set to benefit and bless us, and in light of all we know about the design for our final destiny —"For behold, this is my work and my glory; to bring to pass the immortality and eternal life of man"—the promises for our eternal future are exciting and reassuring. In complete harmony with the principle of free agency, the Lord has reached out to us in an effort to draw us to Him, which is His way, never through force but by persuasion. And this is significant because, while our eternal joy, happiness, and complete fulfillment depend on our coming unto and following Him, we have the personal responsibility, to the greatest extent of our ability, to *choose* to bring these wonderful things about for ourselves because of the nature of the second provision of the Atonement. This is not a completely free gift, as is the resurrection, but must be partly earned, and justly so, since we are responsible for our own violation of law.

We know that although Christ has already mercifully paid the penalty—suffered the consequences—for the wrong-doing for which we will be held accountable, our actual saving from these wrongs is conditional. It depends on our *choice* to willingly humble ourselves, come unto Christ, believe on and obey Him, and be converted to Him and to divine truth. It is conditioned upon our *choosing* to continuously repent for transgressions committed or for those we might yet commit and to live righteously on earth. Thus we can earn the right to be with our Heavenly Father again forever.

But let's go back again to that "merciful payment" made by Christ, those "consequences suffered for our wrongdoing." We must be very sure that, to the best of our abilities, we truly appreciate and understand what that payment and those consequences were. Just what was that great gift of mercy? In reality, of course, there is no possible way, at least on this earth, that we could ever fully comprehend that greatest of gifts. For our task here, nevertheless, we can say that in spite of all our choices and all the arduous efforts we might make to repent and to live worthy lives, in spite of the fact that we are, with our agency, directly responsible for doing these things, no matter how difficult or painful they might be, we are completely unable to be redeemed without His help.

The Father and the Son have eternal respect for man's agency and the tremendous worth of each individual ever created as a child of a divine Father. They have full understanding of our divinely inherited capacities and potential. It is interesting to note that because of these facts, neither the Father nor the Son will ever do anything for us that in their wise judgment they know we can do for ourselves. Then take into account that mercy is partly defined as doing something for another that he cannot do for himself. It is significant, to me, that these two principles, mercy and our own God-given independence and responsibility in combination, put great emphasis on the degree of, first, our great need of Christ's mercy and, second, the tremendous ability He has to give it. If we cannot fully restore and redeem ourselves after all our work and the painstaking care of the Father and Son to allow us every chance to prove our abilities by our own efforts, then how magnificent, incomprehensible, and far-reaching must be the principle of divine mercy and our need for it.

The following anecdotes illustrate man's vital need to put forth every effort toward his own redemption but that that redemption can be met only as he reaches out to the Lord:

"A man walking along the road happens to fall into a pit so deep and dark that he cannot climb to the surface and regain his freedom. How can he save himself from his predicament? Not by any exertion on his part, for there is no means of escape in the pit. He calls for help and some kindly disposed soul, hearing his cries for relief, hastens to his assistance and, by lowering a ladder, gives to him the means by which he may climb again to the surface of the earth." (Author's recollection of a story told by David O. McKay.)

Of course he will remain in the pit if he doesn't make the effort to climb the ladder.

President McKay tells a similar story:

"One day a group of small boys were swimming. Perhaps it would be more accurate to say, they were learning to swim; for none could take more than a few strokes. Just below them a short distance down the stream was a treacherous hole much beyond their depth. Into this, either through bravado or accident, one daring youngster either plunged or fell. He became helpless to save himself; and for a moment his companions were powerless to aid him. Fortunately, one with presence of mind and quick action jerked a long stick from a willow fence and held one end of it toward the drowning lad. The latter grasped it, held on tightly, and was saved.

"All the boys declared that the venturesome lad owed his life to the boy who furnished the means of rescue.

"This is undoubtedly the fact; yet in spite of the means furnished him, if the lad had not taken advantage of it, if he had not put forth all the personal effort at his command, he would have drowned, notwithstanding the heroic act of his comrade." (*Instructor,* January 1955.)

Isn't it interesting that either one of the acts in these stories without the other would have meant disaster. That mercy which the Lord has already given will be effective only if we do our parts, and turned around, no matter how hard we work, we cannot succeed without His help.

Elder LeGrand Richards gives a wonderful example of the point I'm making:

"No matter how much land [a farmer] owns, he cannot expect to reap unless he sows. But when the farmer has prepared his land and sowed his seed, cultivated and irrigated the land, and harvested the crop, is he then entitled to all the credit? He did all the work and is entitled to reap as he has sowed, and the result of his effort will be his reward. But no matter how hard he may have worked, he could not have harvested his crop through his own effort, since there are other factors to be considered:

"1. Who provided the fertile soil?

"2. Who put the germ of life into the seeds he planted?

"3. Who caused the sun to warm the soil, causing the seed to germinate and grow?

"4. Who caused the rain to fall or the snows to fill the watersheds to give drink to his growing crops?

"None of these things could the farmer have done or supplied for himself. They represent the free gift of grace, and yet the farmer will reap as he has sowed." (*A Marvelous Work and a Wonder* [Salt Lake City: Deseret Book Co., 1976] p. 266.)

In all our talk about violation of law and our personal responsibility for it, it is important to realize that there is a difference between acting with knowledge and acting in ignorance, and we learn that we will not be held accountable for those misdemeanors committed without understanding. Elder James E. Talmage, a former member of the Council of the Twelve, gave this explanation:

> According to the technical definition of sin it consists in the violation of law, and in this strict sense sin may be committed inadvertently or in ignorance. It is plain, however, from the scriptural doctrine of human responsibility and the unerring justice of God, that in his transgressions as in his righteous deeds man will be judged according to his ability to comprehend and obey law. To him who has never been made acquainted with a higher law the requirements of that law do not apply in their fulness. For sins committed without knowledge—that is, for laws violated in ignorance—a propitiation [a way] has been provided in the atonement wrought through the sacrifice of the Savior; and sinners of this class do not stand condemned, but shall be given opportunity yet to learn and to accept or reject the principles of the Gospel. (*The Articles of Faith* [Salt Lake City: The Church of Jesus Christ of Latter-day Saints, 1977], p. 58.)

These passages of scripture give added meaning:

> Wherefore, he has given a law; and where there is no law given there is no punishment; and where there is no punishment there is no condemnation; and where there is no condemnation the mercies of the Holy One of Israel have claim upon them, because of the atonement; for they are delivered by the power of him.
>
> For the atonement satisfieth the demands of his justice upon all those who have not the law given to them, that they are delivered from that awful monster, death and hell, and the devil, and the lake of fire and brimstone, which is endless torment; and they are restored to that God who gave them breath, which is the Holy One of Israel.
>
> But wo unto him that has the law given, yea, that has all the commandments of God, like unto us, and that transgresseth them, and that wasteth the days of his probation, for awful is his state! (2 Nephi 9:25–27.)

Then this:

> Nevertheless, there are those among you who have sinned exceedingly; yea, even all of you have sinned; but verily I say unto you, beware from henceforth, and refrain from sin, lest sore judgments fall upon your heads.
>
> For of him unto whom much is given much is required; and he who sins against the greater light shall receive the greater condemnation. (D&C 82:2–3.)

For many, the seriousness and seeming finality of expressions in scripture such as "that awful state," "greater condemnation," "that awful monster, death and hell," and "endless torment," which conditions actually indicate a state of mind, have caused such a sense of discouragement and helplessness that the very saving force of repentance has often been rendered useless in their lives.

The positive state of eternal life, which we can partially earn and of which we have such secure promise, does exist, and repentance is available as the Lord has so aptly reassured us:

> Come unto me, all ye that labour and are heavy laden, and I will give you rest.
>
> Take my yoke upon you, and learn of me; for I am meek and lowly in heart: and ye shall find rest unto your souls.
>
> For my yoke is easy, and my burden is light. (Matthew 11:28–30.)

Eternal life, that highest degree possible for man's attainment and which he earns through his repentance and worthy and righteous living, that state in which he has the blessing of life in the presence of his Heavenly Father, is called by various titles. These different titles, here again, are used at times to mean things other than the highest degree of glory. Terms that I have included to define this exalted state are the *kingdom of God, exaltation, eternal life, life eternal,* and the *celestial kingdom.*

There are other lesser degrees or kingdoms of personal attainment within which other souls will find their places, those places justly deserved according to each individual's conformance to eternal law (see D&C 76).

However, we know and understand a great deal about our Heavenly Father's plan for us. We know something of His and Christ's incomprehensible love for us, and of the sacrifices they have made in our behalf. We know that countless provisions and efforts have been made by them for our benefit. We are also aware that there are great and unique freedoms and opportunities which will be ours in the kingdom of God. Therefore it would seem inconceivable that we would feel adequate fulfillment anywhere else but in the state of eternal life with our Father.

Then, too, considering the decision we all made in that premortal period of our full understanding and the joy and rejoicing we felt in it, is it possible that in our mortal forgetting we would overlook the choicest blessings that would be possible to experience? This is a sobering thought to ponder.

Why Jesus Christ as Savior

With the human limits of our finite knowledge and mental capacity, it is impossible to completely comprehend the purpose and process of the Atonement. However, to understand what we are able to grasp is to acquire a thrilling, overcoming appreciation, a humility, indeed an awe of both the Father and the Son. It allows us more easily to relate to the depths of emotion shown by many as they have attempted to express their testimonies, love, and discipleship of Deity.

What we do understand is that whatever the laws that needed to be respected, a redemption had to be made for mankind because of Adam's purposeful violation of one of those laws. This occurred so that first he and then we, through him, could become mortal. With perfect knowledge of all involved, both of the pertaining laws and man's ultimate destiny, and within the limits of those laws, God the Father outlined a course to make this redemption come to pass.

On a very human level and in a very small way, we might compare the necessity of working with law to the process we go through to get to a designated place by airplane. Though an effective and speedy method of transportation, air travel does have its limitations. Some airlines fly to the east and some to the west, and others go other places. The airlines, themselves, are subject to various situations, including all kinds of weather conditions that directly or indirectly affect us in turn. And all lines have very definite flight schedules which must be adhered to for the sake of efficiency and continuity. In order, then, for us to get where we want to go, there are many factors that have to be taken into account. In the process we are sometimes caused great inconvenience: our flights are laid over, we are transferred during travel from one airline to another, sometimes missing flights and often arriving late at our destination, sometimes without our luggage, I might add. But we continue to fly because it's the best way, at present, to accomplish our purposes, in spite of our occasional sacrifices.

To accomplish the Father's purpose for mankind, only a God could atone for Adam's and man's transgressions. Christ had already been chosen by Heavenly Father in the Council in Heaven to perform that role, and so to make Christ's mission, His sacrifice, possible, the Father prepared His Son for it before He was born into His earth life. Speaking of Christ's voluntary sacrifice, Elder James E. Talmage wrote:

> Though born of a mortal mother, he was begotten in the flesh by an immortal Father; and so combined within His being the capacity to die, and the power to hold death indefinitely in abeyance. He gave up His life; it was not taken from Him against his will. (*The Articles of Faith*, p. 79.)

Jesus Himself said:

> Therefore doth my Father love me, because I lay down my life, that I might take it again. No man taketh it from me, but I lay it down of myself. I have power to lay it down, and I have power to take it again. (John 10:17–18.)

And He also testified:

> For as the Father hath life [immortal] in himself; so hath he
> given to the Son to have life [immortal] in himself; And hath
> given him authority to execute judgment also, because he is
> the Son of man (John 5:26–27).

And further, we must assume that, because of the key factor of free agency, He had the power and the right to choose,
which His Father allowed Him to do. Though Jesus' mission
was already prepared for and foreordained to come about,
Heavenly Father did not force it upon Him, but in absolute respect for His agency, allowed His Son to exercise that same
agency.

The choice He made has great significance. He undoubtedly recognized and accepted His singular preparation for the
role. Being perfectly aware of the personal physical and mental sacrifice He would be called upon to endure, He willingly
volunteered or offered Himself to become the Redeemer of
mankind. And, significant, also, was the Father's acceptance
of His offer. Being fully knowledgeable, Himself, of Christ's
coming ordeal, he faced suffering and sacrifice of His own by
permitting and realizing the sacrifice of His beloved Son in
whom He was well pleased.

Perhaps we can sense a deeper meaning of the words "he
gave his only begotten Son" (John 3:16).

There are other reasons why Christ was qualified to be
our Savior. He was the only person who ever lived on earth
who did not sin, therefore he had nothing from which to repent. He tells us in his own words:

> And he that sent me is with me: the Father hath not left
> me alone; for *I do always those things that please him* (John
> 8:29; italics added).

This purity and innocence made him a worthy sacrifice
for the sins of others.

Another fact that undoubtedly pleased His Father was that
as Christ lived in the premortal life He patterned Himself after

His Father, He became "like unto God." This, of course, would be a necessary attribute of the Savior. We are told also that not only did He love His Father deeply and supported and obeyed Him in all things but, "I am one in the Father, as the Father is one in me, that we may be one" (D&C 35:2).

So we see the significance of the words of scripture that testify of the singular nature of Christ, His mission, and His sacrifice:

> Behold, he offereth himself a sacrifice for sin, to answer the ends of the law, unto all those who have a broken heart and a contrite spirit; and *unto none else can the ends of the law be answered* (2 Nephi 2:7; italics added).

And we also read:

> Behold, Jesus Christ is the name which is given of the Father, and there is none other name given whereby man can be saved (D&C 18:23).

As we conclude this portion of our discourse on the Atonement and its accompanying facets, I add the testimony to these truths of President David O. McKay. This testimony, given in a letter to his son, lends great insight into this most valuable of all principles and events:

" 'In the beginning' whenever that was, man found himself shut out from God's eternal presence. He remembered little and in time would have remembered nothing of his associations with eternal beings. . . . Earth and earthly things were everything to him. When he became hungry, it was earth that satisfied him; when he became thirsty, it was an earthly element that quenched his thirst; when he became cold, it was the skins of animals that protected him and kept him warm; or it was the great moving luminary in the sky that shed his genial rays on man's chilly limbs.

"When he sought comfort in repose, it was from the trees, or from skins of animals, or from vegetation of the earth that gave him a downy bed. In short, the earth became not only man's 'foster mother,' she was to him the source of his very existence.

"Self-preservation became not only the first law, but I can imagine, the only law he knew. As the race increased, and the struggle for existence became more acute, selfishness and strife would manifest themselves. Man would struggle with man for supremacy or for the best things nature could offer for the prolongation or the comforts of life. Thus would man become 'carnal, sensual, and devilish, by nature.' (Alma 42:6–13)

"Now, what was there in man to lead him up to a Godlike life? The divinity within him, I grant you, would be ever urging him to rise above himself. But his reverence for the Infinite could express itself only in worship of the manifestations of Divine power—the *sun*, the *moon*, the *thunder*, the *lightning*, the cataract, the volcano, etc.

"How significant is that passage, then, which says, 'By grace are ye saved through faith; and that not of yourselves; it is the gift of God.' The Lord revealed to man the Gospel, and one of the very first commandments given superseded in essence the self-preservation law. It was the law of sacrifice. The effect of this was that the best the earth produced, the best specimen in the flock or herd should not be used for self, but for God. It was God, not the earth, whom man should worship. How this simple test of sacrifice affected the divine nature as well as the carnal in man, the story of Cain and Abel graphically and appropriately illustrates. For one, the best the 'firstlings of the flock' was all too poor as a means of expressing his love and appreciation of the revelation of life that God had given; for the other he would go through the form because God had commanded, but he would keep the best for himself.

"And so through the ages, this eternal conflict between the divine life of service and the earth life of carnal and sensual and selfish indulgence and ease continued. Millions lived and died believing that the whole purpose of life is to get and possess what earth has to give, never comprehending that the whole purpose of life is to give.

"Then in the Meridian of time came the Savior of man,

toward whose coming man in the morning of life had looked forward, and upon whose life man in the evening of life should look in retrospect. In the meridian of the earth's history came the Son of Man declaring the eternal truth so opposed to the promises of the earth, that he that would save his life must lose it.

"And in His brief stay upon earth, how perfectly He exemplified this truth. He owned no land. He owned no house; for He had not where to lay His head. 'The foxes have holes, and the birds of the air have nests; but the son of man hath not where to lay his head.' (Matthew 8:20)

"His was a life of unselfish service—always helping those who were living incompletely to live completely—whether the incomplete living was caused by a physical defect such as blindness or deafness, or whether through a moral defect such as the woman taken in sin—His mission was to give them life.

"Now, my dear son, can you not carry this thought a little further and apply it even to the sacrificing of His life, to the shedding of His blood? Man's life is not dependent upon what this earth can give—his body, yes, but that is only the house in which man lives—but the spirit, the real man is above the selfish and the sensual, and seeks for its life and happiness the things which are eternal—faith, virtue, knowledge, temperance, Godliness, brotherliness, charity.

"In His life and death, therefore, Christ not only fulfilled the law of sacrifice but He fulfilled every conceivable condition necessary for man to know in order to rise or progress from earthly life to eternal life. 'And I, if I be lifted up from the earth, will draw all men unto me.' (John 12:32)

"In this I think I glimpse, though ever so dimly, a reason for Christ's shedding His blood—in addition to the one generally offered for the redemption of man from the Fall. I confess that the latter has moved me less than the realization that in His life He lived for His fellow men, and in His death, he triumphed over all earthly elements, over the power of Death, Hell and the Evil One, and arose from the grave, an eternal Being—our Guide, our Saviour, our God." ("The Atonement," *Instructor,* March 1959, pp. 65–66.)

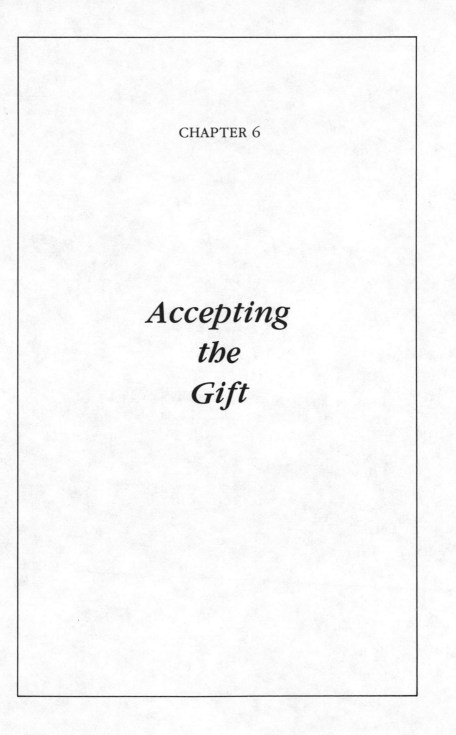

CHAPTER 6

Accepting
the
Gift

Paul, before becoming the Apostle, and according to the life-style and standards of his time, had lived, as he claimed he had, a highly moral life. Facing the foes who accused him of gross sin, he said what you and I are inclined to say at times, that he could find nothing wrong in himself, even though, he added, he could not be his own judge, that that would be the right of God the Father. But later, as he reflected upon the Savior's crucifixion and saw himself in the light of Christ's teachings, this was what he had to say of himself: "Christ Jesus came into the world to save sinners; of whom I am chief" (1 Timothy 1:15).

Recognizing Our Transgressions

How easy it is, as close to ourselves as we are, to overlook, look around, behind, and in every other direction except straight at those things in our lives that we call errors, transgressions, wrongdoings, and sins. Yet how foolish it is to do anything else when our entire earthly joy, which was intended, our happiness, success, peace of mind, and eventual and eternal future depend on it.

If the question were asked, most of us could readily define wrongdoing or sin as those acts committed that are contrary to that which is right or true, or as James states: "To him that knoweth to do good, and doeth it not, to him it is sin" (James 4:17). Many of us also know that there are different kinds of wrongdoing, acts both small and large, those of omission as well as commission, those done knowingly and willfully and those done in ignorance or innocence.

And we can hardly ignore the reality of the inevitable and various natural consequences that plague us as the result of our choices and actions. They range anywhere from small inconveniences to embarrassments, then hurt feelings, damage to others' self-esteem, and on up the scale to serious moral and physical disasters. Also, we all, if we are honest with ourselves, have lived with and have come to appreciate not only the moral and physical effects of error but also the more private mental and emotional pains felt because of our own transgressions — oppressive guilt, self-hate, great disappointment as we see ourselves fall below our own standards and expectations, loss of our own self-esteem, and so forth.

Less easily identified and accepted by us, and, at that, often with great discomfort and defensiveness, are our rationalizing of error, somehow justifying and making excuses for ourselves; our lack of recognition of our mistakes in the first place; and the blame we place on others and on situations and conditions to avoid taking responsibility for those mistakes.

Since the whole message and promise of the second phase of the Atonement hinges on wrongdoing and the challenge and necessity of overcoming it, it would be well to take a few minutes to think about it. The most obvious reason that comes to my mind for overcoming sin is so that we can bring about a change or reformation in our lives, an upgrade in our actions and thoughts. We have certainly learned from all the teachings of truth that change is the desired outcome and goal of repentance. Repentance, as well as continual righteousness, in turn, are the admonitions given us through all scripture by which we can gain eternal life. It is clear that in order to accomplish the one, repentance, we must do away with the other, sin.

Why do we make mistakes, create problems for ourselves and others, or sometimes become destructive to man and property?

Consider our exposure in earth life to the conditions of opposition, not only the many good influences but also the great numbers of less than desirable factors from which we may choose. Take into account man's comparably few years on earth during which he has an opportunity to learn, and the vast amount of what there is *to* learn. Think that we were born into earth life in complete ignorance of all of this—of all we ever *did* know—and of how dependent we are on the particular and different kinds of environments in which we were raised. We've learned much or little, and some of that is untruth. Is it any wonder that we struggle with transgression?

It is, in fact, inevitable that mistakes will be made and laws broken. I've often wondered if it wasn't God's intention all along that we learn that way, the hard way; that we learn respect for law by our own mistakes, painful as they are. Apparently it's a good method, because it seems that when we hurt enough we tend to seek better ways to act and to solve our problems, and we try to avoid repeating the unsuccessful behavior.

When I was a young man I had a priests quorum advisor who liked to teach his class new thoughts each week. Every Sunday at the end of our quorum meeting he would give us a gem thought, profound but easy to remember. And every time we came to class he would ask each of us to give him a new inspirational thought that we had found during the week. These thoughts have never been forgotten. I used them all the way through the army, through college, and, as an officer in the Church, I am still quoting them.

I would like, as did my teacher, Charles B. Stewart, to give you a few such short but meaningful thoughts that give added insight into peoples' feelings and experiences with their offenses:

Folks do not get to heaven on goodness who were good for lack of opportunity to do bad.

My sins don't cause me apprehensions;
For I've the best of alibis:
It's simply that my good intentions
Refuse to materialize.

When you see sin ripening in your neighbor's garden, look out for the seeds in your own.

Few serve Satan better than sleeping saints.

The deadliest sin were the consciousness of no sin.

Or, to put it another way:

If you think you have no faults, that makes another one.

Every sin is a mistake as well as a wrong, and the epitaph for the sinner is, Thou fool.

That which we call sin in others is experiment to us.

For where your treasure is, there will your heart be also.

How do you spend your time? Looking for a way or looking for an excuse?

No man becomes fully evil at once; but suggestions bringeth on indulgence; indulgence, delight; delight, consent; consent, endeavor; endeavor, excuse; excuse, defense; defense, obstinacy; obstinacy, boasting; boasting, a seared conscience and a reprobate mind.

Bad men hate sin through fear of punishment. Good men hate sin through their love of virtue.

Your conscience may not keep you from doing wrong, but it can surely keep you from enjoying it.

Sin is not hurtful because it's forbidden, but it is forbidden because it is hurtful.

It is not only what we do but also what we do not do for which we are accountable.

Sin is to be overcome, not so much by direct opposition to it as [by] cultivating opposite principles. Would you kill the weed in your garden, plant it with good seed; if the ground be well occupied there would be less need of the hoe.

I never cease to marvel at the hundreds of profound thoughts given on all principles of truth and man's experiences by great, humble, observant, and experienced men and women. It proves to me, and comfortingly so, that all through the ages of time mankind relives the same problems and continues to find that truth is the path toward the recognition and the solving of those problems.

A word of caution as we go about the much needed identification of error in ourselves. There are times when we become so anxious for righteousness, so eager to bring about change for the better, to be honest with ourselves, which is right, that it is possible to lose our perspective. We find ourselves taking blame for every negative thing that happens, constantly finding fault with our behavior or actions and berating ourselves, losing positive attitudes, and questioning our self-worth and self-esteem. This can become so depressing that it squelches all motivation to try. At these times we cease to be properly and appropriately kind and fair with ourselves. There are, of course, very fine lines here, and it is easy to go to great extremes in either direction. We can become so negative, feel so guilty, and sometimes become so unreasonable in our self-expectations that it can be defeating to us. Or we can become so easygoing in our attempt to be fair with ourselves that we rationalize far past good sense. The desired goal is the great principle of balance by which we are able to honestly accept ourselves as makers of mistakes and errors and yet still rightly see ourselves continually learning, over-coming, and striving to reach the greatest heights of worthy living. In this more positive attitude, we are best prepared to look at the principle of repentance properly; repentance, that great provision given by our Father for such life situations. We can then feel deep, sincere sorrow and remorse for sin, have strong, confident commitment to action, and follow with change.

Remember, too, the Lord has told us that when we truly repent, He will remember our sin no more. This is a comfort-ing, reassuring, and important promise to us, but it sometimes has caused confusion. There are those who have sincerely re-pented, changed, but still question whether they have ac-tually been forgiven because their own remembrance of the wrong still exists in their minds. The Lord promised us that *He* would forget the sin, not that *we* would forget. At this point it is our responsibility to put the unfortunate event in the back of our minds by forgiving ourselves. This will bring about a gradual effect, not of complete forgetting, but of feel-ing the peace that we have done all that was expected of us. Time will then become the healing balm.

We must learn to forgive ourselves as well as others be-cause, as children of a divine Father, we have great need to feel strong, personal worth and esteem, to honor and appre-ciate our divine inheritance. That also is why we have such a deep need to feel forgiveness from our Heavenly Father and from each other. To feel clean again, redeemed once more, capable and acceptable still, is vital to our ability to function responsibly on earth.

Not only we but our family members, our neighbors, our friends, our business associates, everyone with whom we come in contact, need this same forgiveness and for the same reason. The Savior has given much counsel on this point.

He has taught repeatedly the great importance of being willing to forgive others if we ourselves would ask forgive-ness of our Father.

In one instance He said:

For if ye forgive men their trespasses, your heavenly Father will also forgive you:

But if ye forgive not men their trespasses, neither will your Father forgive your trespasses (Matthew 6:14–15).

Another time Peter asked Him:

Lord, how oft shall my brother sin against me, and I forgive him? till seven times?

And Jesus gave him this answer:

I say not unto thee, Until seven times: but, Until seventy times seven (Matthew 18:21–22).

Actually there is no limit to how many times we must forgive.

Today our Heavenly Father counsels us further:

Wherefore, I say unto you, that ye ought to forgive one another; for he that forgiveth not his brother his trespasses standeth condemned before the Lord; for there remaineth in him the greater sin.

I, the Lord, will forgive whom I will forgive, but of you it is required to forgive all men. (D&C 64:9–10.)

A question and a thought about our own forgiveness from the Father. What good would it do for Him to extend forgiveness to us for our wrongdoing if we had not humbled our hearts and become repentant, even if He saw fit to do so under those conditions? Without feeling real sorrow for those things we had done, we would be completely unable to accept that gift or even want it, because we had not yet turned from the error of our ways. Heavenly Father forgives when we are humble and sincere in our remorse and are doing something about it. Then we will have earned and can receive his forgiveness.

This condition of humility, or lack of it, however, does not necessarily follow in our requirement to forgive others.

We apparently are not excused from that duty, regardless of others' feelings or acts.

The principle of forgiveness is vital to the Lord and to each of us, though to actually forgive, even ourselves, is not always easy. Usually others' small offenses toward us are not hard to forgive and forget. Everyone makes mistakes. The times when forgiveness is difficult, however, are when damages are great and we are angry, or when the hurts are deep and we are wounded emotionally. Hopefully, understanding somewhat the causes of man's sinning, the basic goodness of his nature, and our own need of forgiveness, along with having great faith and courage, will help make that most important law easier to follow.

For some, however, there are those extreme situations when acts have been committed against us or particular deeds have affected us so very painfully that there seems to be no possibility that we could ever forgive. Neither reason nor understanding alone are sufficient to move us. Such was the experience of Corrie ten Boom, the amazing and courageous Dutch woman of such tremendous faith, who survived months in Nazi concentration camps under the most terrible circumstances. Her determination to serve her God and to bring comfort, encouragement, faith, and hope to her fellow prisoners during this period brought blessings to herself as well as to countless others. Christ's Spirit and words were her guide, and His strength sustained her.

Finally, after her release from the camps and after the end of World War II, she traveled all over the world lecturing and testifying of God's love and care, the truth of His teachings, and the need for forgiveness on the part of thousands as a means of healing the world from the devastation of war.

One night after a lecture at a church service in Munich, Germany, she saw coming toward her one of her former prison guards, and suddenly all the months of horror were upon her once more. In her own words she recounts the experience and her incredible challenge, teaching us all the power of the Father in times of tremendous need.

He came up to me as the church was emptying, beaming and bowing. "How grateful I am for your message, *Fraulein*," he said. . . .

His hand was thrust out to shake mine. And I, who had preached so often to the people in Bloemendaal the need to forgive, kept my hand at my side.

Even as the angry, vengeful thoughts boiled through me, I saw the sin of them. Jesus Christ had died for this man; was I going to ask for more? Lord Jesus, I prayed, forgive me and help me to forgive him.

I tried to smile, I struggled to raise my hand. I could not. I felt nothing, not the slightest spark of warmth or charity. And so again I breathed a silent prayer. Jesus, I cannot forgive him. Give me Your forgiveness.

As I took his hand the most incredible thing happened. From my shoulder along my arm and through my hand a current seemed to pass from me to him, while into my heart sprang a love for this stranger that almost overwhelmed me.

And so I discovered that it is not on our forgiveness any more than on our goodness that the world's healing hinges, but on His. When He tells us to love our enemies, He gives, along with the command, the love itself. (From Corrie ten Boom, with John and Elizabeth Sherrill, *The Hiding Place*, p. 238. Copyright © 1971. Used by permission of Bantam Books.)

To the side of fairness in self-judgment, again, I'd like to interject a bit of fact that I have learned through hours of counseling hundreds of distressed souls. I have found that wrongdoing and sinning often occur where there is much deep need for secure feelings of worth.

Lives and involvements may be very meaningless and mundane; value systems may have failed, if, in fact, they ever existed; self-confidence and fulfillment, to say nothing of happiness or even peace of mind, may be very inadequate — all of these leaving great feelings of unworth, unworthiness, and unacceptability.

Such circumstances must have prevailed in the following situation of a majestic lion, a king of the jungle.

The story is told of this great beast, who had the strength, courage, and boldness normal to all such beasts, but who, for some reason, believed that he was really a lamb, or in other words, had no proper knowledge and acceptance of his real worth.

He went into the jungle fearing and trembling because lambs don't usually survive under such wild circumstances. He wondered whatever he would do to save himself from inevitable destruction. Finally he hit upon an idea. He went out, found a lion's skin and draped it over himself, thus "proving" to himself that he was what he wanted to be, in fact, what he already was. (From a lecture given by Sterling G. Ellsworth at a regional conference of the Oregon Elementary School Principals' Association, 2 April 1966.)

I think many of us, in our own way, find our lions' skins and use them frequently, as shown by our various behaviors.

Once again, however, though the line between the principles of humble honesty and loving fairness is very fine, it is definitely *there,* making the principles on both sides of the balance equal in importance. One may say a criminal might be judged more leniently because of the reasons he became a criminal, that he has rights as a free agent, yet in spite of his rights, he must still be stopped in his crimes. He does not have the right to victimize society. And the Lord, then, may be his final judge. A statement has been made about this thought:

> Sin has always been an ugly word, but it has been made so in a new sense over the last half-century. It has been made not only ugly but passé. People are no longer sinful, they are only immature or underprivileged or frightened or, more particulary, "sick."

How fortunate we are that new insight and understanding have been brought to light concerning man's behavior and his emotional nature, functions, and needs. Yet, I believe, we do a disservice to all those who commit wrong by not expecting them to be responsible for their acts. And, in a personal vein, we cannot completely turn our backs on our own various wrongdoings in order to preserve our feelings of self-worth, which could not be preserved anyway under those circumstances. Wickedness was never happiness nor does it ever bring peace of mind or feelings of worth. Again, the principle of balance and the word *caution.*

Thinking back to the account of Paul the Apostle, remember that John, another Apostle, also wrote:

> If we say that we have no sin, we deceive ourselves, and the truth is not in us (1 John 1:8).

And Jesus, Himself, said:

> He that is without sin among you, let him first cast a stone. . . . Go, and sin no more. (John 8:7, 11.)

Repentance

Elder B. H. Roberts, a former member of the First Quorum of the Seventy, in beautiful and poetic language, teaches a masterful lesson about the wonderful encouragement toward repentance that is brought to the hearts of men, as in the case of Paul, when they begin to see and really grasp the reality and truths of God the Father and His Son Jesus Christ and their teachings.

In his own words he explains:

> No sooner does conviction of God's existence, and of the truth of the revelations which he has given of himself, and of his laws, dawn upon the mind, than man becomes conscious of his being a violator of the holy and just laws of heaven. In the days of his unbelief and spiritual darkness he sinned recklessly and wantonly, and without regard to God and often in defiance of him; but when belief takes hold of the mind, and when mere belief begins to ripen into intelligent faith through becoming acquainted with the character of the Deity —when it becomes clear to the understanding that he is the Creator and the sustaining Power of all things; . . . that his

laws are beneficient and good, shaped for the purpose of en-
nobling man and exalting him . . .—how the haughty, rebel-
lious spirit is humbled, the heart softened, and the whole de-
meanor changed! (*The Gospel and Man's Relationship to
Deity*, p. 113.)

From this statement we learn that if repentance is to take
place, if change is to be made, one must first have some
degree of knowledge and assurance of the rightness and
"worthwhileness" of those things he has been turning his
back on or ignoring or of laws that he has been violating. All
the exposure and teaching in the world will not cause a person to try something new, particularly when it comes to
moral behavior, if he sees no personal value or gain in it for
himself.

In the field of education it has been proven over the years
that there are five definite steps that must occur to enable any
kind of learning and change to take place.

1. *Exposure*	One must be presented with a prin-ciple, idea, or fact.
2. *Repetition*	That principle or fact must be re-peated a certain number of times, depending on what it is—many times for complex concepts.
3. *Understanding*	One must come to understand the principle or idea.
4. *Commitment*	If sufficient understanding has been gained, then one is able to accept its truth and commit to doing some-thing about it.
5. *Application*	Adapting a new behavior or concept into one's life occurs only after a commitment is made.

Since the application of principles is our concern here, it
is also well to be aware of the known fact that one will rarely
pursue with diligence and lasting success and satisfaction any

course of action that he doesn't understand and to which he isn't totally committed.

In my own teaching experience, especially with young people, I have found the most success when I try to teach the "why" of a principle or idea. I make an effort to answer the "why" of the inevitable questions that students either put into words or have written all over their faces: "So what?" "How does that fit my life?" "What does that have to do with me?" "That is past history."

Let me illustrate the point by sharing an incident that made a great difference in my life.

I recall so well an experience I had one time as a teenager living in California. In my priests quorum meeting one Sunday morning, our adviser was teaching a lesson on sin and repentance. He made a strong point about the evils and effects of sin in our lives and their lasting influence. Wanting to illustrate his message to impressionable young minds, he produced a brand new piece of lumber which he said represented our innocent and pure lives. He took from his bag a hammer and a large rusty nail, and pointing to the nail, told us that it was like the sins we sometimes commit either purposely or in ignorance.

He then proceeded to drive the nail into the shiny new board with loud, ringing pounds of the hammer. As the nail sank deep into the board, the teacher gave great emphasis to the fact that transgression is like the nail, it quickly and lastingly mars one's personal life.

Commenting on the blessing of repentance that is provided us, he then taught that our sins could be forgiven as a result of Christ's atonement. In order to show the class how repentance works, he started to remove the rusty nail with the claw end of the hammer. He very slowly withdrew it, and as he did so it made an eerie sound: *eeeekk!* Then he said, "Now even though the sin has been forgiven (or the nail removed), notice the effects that remain." He pointed to the hole left in the board.

In some way his illustration didn't seem quite right to me.

Not only didn't it seem right, but it made me quite uncomfortable and discouraged and even a little defensive, thinking that, even if I really was sorry for something I had done, it wouldn't really matter or do any good anyway. I distinctly remember that at the time I somehow felt I didn't want to think about the idea of the nail and the hole at all.

Sometime later, at a church social at the beach, I was running along the wet sand, the water lapping at my feet. Suddenly I stopped, noticing that as I had been running, my footprints were being filled in and wiped completely out by the sand and the water as the waves had covered them. Then for some reason, the example of the nail and the hole came back to me, and I could actually see the comparison between the two ideas. I could grasp the more accurate concept that repentance really does completely wipe away the sin. Finally, that factor of the principle of repentance made sense to me. I have since realized that I was very blessed at the time to be able to put the two examples together and come up with this valuable and positive concept, but even at that tender age this new understanding really helped me to pay more attention to what I was doing every day, and when I did do wrong, I was more willing to try to change something. It really was a great feeling!

The realization and the resulting faith that came that day, in addition to that of other experiences in my youth, has been added upon even more as the years have passed and I have matured and been involved in the serious living of life. How many times that faith has helped to strengthen me toward repentance and how grateful I have been for it! To conclude this personal incident, it would be well to recall once again Heavenly Father's promise that if we truly repent He will remember our sins no more.

Elder Roberts goes on to say that the more understanding we gain about true principles, the more sorrow we feel for wrongdoing. And these feelings do not come only to those who have committed serious offenses but to all of us, even as we are striving to do our best toward righteousness but still see how we might improve our lives further and attain to higher levels of worthiness. It is easy to understand, then, the reality of the truth of the following scriptures:

> Therefore by the deeds of the law there shall no flesh be
> justified [guiltless] in his sight: for by the law is the knowl-
> edge of sin. . . .
> For all have sinned, and come short of the glory of God.
> (Romans 3:20, 23.)

> And behold, when that time cometh, none shall be found
> blameless before God, except it be little children, only
> through repentance and faith on the name of the Lord God
> Omnipotent (Mosiah 3:21).

We are repeatedly given the counsel and the encouragement to "come unto Christ." This is valuable counsel, not
just for the sake of being obedient, but because, by following
this path, we ourselves become the beneficiaries. We do ourselves a great service by thinking and living in harmony with
the reality of true principles. By doing these things, we will
achieve true happiness and peace of mind here on earth because we will receive the positive consequences that we have
earned. At the same time we will be preparing for the great
blessings brought about by the atonement of Jesus Christ.

Man was meant to be free, free to exercise his mind and
will, to choose the course he will follow. Yet, in reality, the
only true freedom we can experience is that which comes
from within the framework of law.

We know that some of the blessings of the Atonement are
conditional, that we must earn them. I sometimes wonder,
however, if we really internalize the fact that the earning of
these blessings must take place every single day we live, that
it must accompany every act we perform, that we cannot wait
until the end. I wonder if we take the time in our days, weeks,
and months for granted; they always come and so, therefore,
they always will, or if the unpredictability of death gives us a
false security, especially in our younger years. Our daily preparations must consist of repenting of former transgression, attempting to avoid additional wrongdoing, and conscien-
tiously living as close to Christ's example as possible. We will
not be perfect, but we will always be working toward that desirable condition.

Consider this wise counsel:

> Yea, I would that ye would come forth and harden not your hearts any longer; for behold, *now is the time and the day* of your salvation; and therefore, if ye will repent and harden not your hearts, immediately shall the great plan of redemption be brought about unto you.
>
> For behold, *this life is the time* for men to prepare to meet God; yea, behold the day of this life is the day for men to perform their labors. (Alma 34:31–32; italics added.)

> . . . Therefore *this life* became a probationary state; . . . a time to prepare for that endless state which has been spoken of by us, which is after the resurrection of the dead (Alma 12:24; italics added).

The Sacrament

As human beings in a world filled with opposition, we are constantly confronted with influences that suggest, urge, and sometimes tempt us to "march to other drums," to face attractions, thoughts, and concepts which are in direct disharmony with truth. Even though opposition is necesary to enable us to have choices, to choose between truth and falsehood, these encounters with undesirable influences sometimes make it easy to waver in our steadfastness. Let me repeat one of our gem thoughts from another chapter.

> Folks do not get to heaven on goodness who were good for lack of opportunity to be bad.

In His mercy our Father has provided us with many safeguards and much assistance to guide, direct, give comfort, reveal truth and knowledge, and keep us close to Him and the principles of truth if we will but take advantage of them. We have the Light of Christ which is given to all men. Also we have the Holy Ghost, who is the Comforter, the revealer of truth, and He who searches our hearts. There are prophets and other leaders to teach His word, and the scriptures from which to teach. Then there is the privilege of continuous revelation and the right to personal communication with our Father through prayer. Important ordinances exist which bring great and special blessings to us, in fact we cannot come unto Christ without them. One of these ordinances is the sacrament of the Lord's Supper. This very special ordinance is so clearly and so closely tied to the Atonement and Christ's sacrifice that it becomes very valuable to us as a remembrance of Him, especially as it is taken each week.

The partaking of the sacrament of the Lord's Supper is one of the most sacred ordinances of the Church. You will recall that on the occasion of the sacrament's institution, the Lord himself attached great importance to it. In that special meeting with his Twelve Apostles in the upper room at Jerusalem, He partook of the Passover with them in accordance with the Jewish practice. Then he took bread and brake it, and said,

> Take, eat; this is my body.
> And he took the cup, and gave thanks, and gave it to them, saying, Drink ye all of it;
> For this is my blood of the new testament, which is shed for many for the remission of sins.
> But I say unto you, I will not drink henceforth of this fruit of the vine, until that day when I drink it new with you in my Father's kingdom. (Matthew 26:26–29.)

The question is sometimes raised: What does the Lord's Supper signify and why is it so sacred? President David O. McKay, in a wonderful editorial, gives us four principles to be gleaned from the sacrament. First, he says:

> You will find . . . that the sacrament is a memorial of Christ's life and death. When we think of his life, we think of sacrifice. Not a moment of his mission on earth did Christ think more of himself than he did of his brethren and of the people whom he came to save, always losing himself for the good of others, and finally giving his life for the redemption of mankind. When we partake of the sacrament in his presence, we

remember him, his life of sacrifice and service; and we are inspired by that thought and memory. There is no progress, no soul growth won in this life without sacrifice.

A second principle associated with the administering of the sacrament is the bond of brotherhood. In the early establishment of the Church of Jesus Christ the brethren met, we are told, often at daybreak, to partake of this sacrament as in the bond of brotherhood, of oneness. . . .

We meet in the brotherhood of Christ, all on the same level, each expressing confidence in the other and all in one another.

[Third,] the partaking of the sacrament indicates also how communion with Christ may be secured. It cannot be obtained by Sunday righteousness and weekday indulgence. It implies that we will "remember" Christ always.

And the fourth great significance is the promise that it is a means of receiving divine guidance. . . .

And what is the blessing? — "That they may always have his Spirit to be with them." (*Improvement Era*, January 1953, pp. 13–14.)

The sacramental service is the ideal time for each of us to meditate and ponder on our lives, our thoughts and actions and responsibilities; to renew the promises and covenants made at the time of baptism, and as part of other important ordinances, and for many, the covenants made in the temple. It is a time to express gratitude for our blessings and sorrow for our weaknesses and errors, and to ask for forgiveness. The taking of the sacrament gives us the opportunity of communication with our Father and rededication to Him and, if partaken of in the spirit of humility, gratitude, and worship, it revitalizes our spirits and provides stimulation toward desirable goals that helps to carry us through all our days.

How truly blessed we are, as children of our Heavenly Father, to feel still another example of His love and concern for us. His "work and His glory" is so all important to Him and to us that both instinctively and purposely, He leaves nothing to chance in His designs and efforts on our behalf.

It is my personal witness and experience that accepting all of the gifts provided us will bring joy and eternal peace to us all.

CHAPTER 7

This One Is Empty

O ne of my first exposures to the divine principle of Christ's atonement and the principle of repentance occurred when I was about twelve years old. Up to my high school age my family resided in one of the southern states. The branch of the Church there was extremely small and did not provide the usual opportunities of activity and involvement for youth. My father and mother fortunately took the time to supplement gospel teaching in special and varied ways. It was in such a setting that my father taught me a great lesson about the atonement of our Lord and Savior.

Baseball, among other sporting activities, consumed much of my early life. This was in an era when there were no Little Leagues or American Legion baseball teams, and neighborhoods used to provide their own teams and then challenge other neighborhoods. These were tough competitions with little supervision. In fact, I have often felt since that time that such contests provided an excellent training ground for my eventual military experiences.

During that period my parents permitted my brothers and me to use our backyard, which was fairly large, for a baseball diamond and other sporting events. The yard was totally fenced in and had a back alley running along the outside of the fence. A large Protestant church backed up to the far side of the alley. The second floor sanctuary of the church had at its front a large stained glass window depicting the Last Supper. The back side of that beautiful window faced our backyard fence, which to us during baseball season was the centerfield fence of our diamond.

This particular Protestant denomination conducted many spiritual revival sessions during the summer months, and one hot summer evening church was in session at the same hour that our neighborhood was involved in a competitive baseball contest in our yard.

I came to bat late in the game and hit an outside pitch with more power than I had ever experienced to that point in my life. The ball cleared the centerfield fence, sailed across the alley and entered the church, some 260 feet away, through the stained glass window. It seemed to this young lad that glass fell for an eternity. The entire field of young athletes scattered in all directions. I believe I might have established an Olympic hurdling record as I cleared a rather high hedge separating our house from that of the neighbors.

When I returned home some time later, I discovered that my parents had two visitors from the local parish. One was the minister and the other, his assistant. As my father called me into their presence and introduced me to them, I was somewhat startled to learn that they seemed to know from which house the baseball had come. The two men had told my father that while they were holding their evening service, a baseball had shattered the stained glass window at the front of the sanctuary.

My father put his arm around my shoulder, patted me on the head, and said, "This is a good boy. He would not purposely do harm to another's property." He then invited all of us to take a seat. He apologized for the incident and asked the two religious representatives how much it would cost to replace the stained glass window. He was told that it would be in the neighborhood of five hundred dollars! Now, this was during the time of the Great Depression when funds were hard to come by, and to me five hundred dollars sounded like the national debt.

My father then asked the ministers if they believed in the principle of Christ's atonement. They seemed somewhat puzzled but answered yes! He then said, "In our church [which name he identified] we believe that through the atonement of Christ all mankind may be saved by obedience to the laws and ordinances of the gospel." Then he briefly explained that the atonement of Christ has a twofold effect. First it saves all mankind from the fall or transgression of Adam by means of the resurrection, which is universal. That resurrection of the dead is for *all* mankind, the unjust as well as the just, and because of it we will live forever. He pointed out that the second effect opens the way for our individual salvation. In this way we may acquire for ourselves a remission of personal sins, sins that are the result of our own acts and that require repentance and forgiveness. He further pointed out that by living righteously and by obeying the laws and ordinances of the gospel, each of us could again regain the presence of our Heavenly Father.

Then he briefly explained our belief that prior to living here upon the earth, we existed in a premortal life and that we came to earth for a divine purpose. One day all mankind will die and will pass through a physical death, making the Atonement necessary in order that our bodies and spirits can be rejoined and so that we can regain our Father's presence. He also explained that the atonement of Christ involved two very important principles: justice and mercy.

In outlining these principles for our visitors (and I now understand that he was really teaching me), he pointed out that justice demands rightness and obedience to law, and that mercy is best defined as something that is done for another that he cannot do for himself.

He quickly pointed out that, while I had unintentionally broken a rule (the law) and that that law, or justice, demanded payment, I was not in a position to pay for a five hundred dollar stained glass window on an allowance of twenty-five cents a week. My father then said he would pay the price since I could not and that, by so doing he, as my father, would be doing for me what I could not do for myself (mercy). Then, taking his checkbook from his coat pocket, he wrote out a check for the amount of the window.

After this explanation to the minister and his assistant, and to me, he then turned and instructed me as to what my role in all of this was to be. He told me that out of love for us, Christ had been willing to extend mercy to all—but only on the condition that people would feel real sorrow for their mistakes and be willing to make up for their wrong in the best way they could, and that this would be my responsibility as well.

He explained that at my age I was fully able to understand what I had done and that even though it had been an accident, which I had certainly not intended to cause, I needed to appreciate the seriousness of what had happened and the extensive damage that had been done. Then I needed to feel sincerely sorry and express those feelings to the two men. After that he and I would sit down and work out a plan, involving my twenty-five cents a week, to make amends and to help pay the debt. And both of us did exactly that—he did his part and I did mine.

This experience made a deep impression on me; I recall that even at that young age I felt gratitude for the things I had just learned about the Atonement and the role that Jesus Christ had in it and for the new understanding I had gained. I have never forgotten the incident.

Through the wonderful principle of mercy, Christ paid the price that we could not. Following His agony in the Garden of Gethsemane and on the cross, His body was taken down, was wrapped in linen, and was placed in a new tomb. Then Luke further records:

> Now upon the first day of the week, very early in the morning, they came unto the sepulchre, bringing the spices which they had prepared, and certain others with them.
>
> And they found the stone rolled away from the sepulchre.
>
> And they entered in, and found not the body of the Lord Jesus.
>
> And it came to pass, as they were much perplexed thereabout, behold, two men stood by them in shining garments:

And as they were afraid, and bowed down their faces to the earth, they said unto them, Why seek ye the living among the dead?

He is not here, but is risen: remember how he spake unto you when he was yet in Galilee,

Saying, The Son of man must be delivered into the hands of sinful men, and be crucified, and the third day rise again.

And they remembered his words,

And returned from the sepulchre, and told all these things unto the eleven, and to all the rest. (Luke 24:1–9.)

And then (as recorded in Matthew 28:6) three of the greatest words ever spoken:

He is risen!

It was Christ, Himself, who had testified:

I am the resurrection, and the life: he that believeth in me, though he were dead, yet shall he live:

And whosoever liveth and believeth in me shall never die (John 11:25–26).

I recall the words that President Harold B. Lee spoke at the funeral of one of the Twelve Apostles. He said:

In 1956 a guide in the Holy Land led Adam S. Bennion to the tomb [which had belonged] to Joseph of Arimathaea in the days when Jesus lived and in which Jesus was entombed after the crucifixion. As the guide stood there he said: "There are many tombs of great men to be found all over the earth, but this one is different from any of the others — this one is empty!" (Harold B. Lee at funeral for Adam S. Bennion.)

This is my personal witness also. As surely as anything I know, I know that Jesus Christ lived and was and is our Savior. He died. He was resurrected. His tomb is empty. It will always be empty! And just as surely as I know that He rose from His tomb, we will all do the same. Such was the eternal plan.

For just as Job raised the question, "If a man die, shall he live again?" he also answered with his testimony:

> For I know that my redeemer liveth, and that he shall stand at the latter day upon the earth:
> And though after my skin worms destroy this body, yet in my flesh shall I see God (Job 19:25–26).

CHAPTER 8

Family Traditions
and
Reunions

As a youngster I recall so well the many family traditions my brothers and I enjoyed. Sundays were always special. Every Sunday morning our mother would make pancakes. Then came the ritual of reading the funny papers before getting ready for Church. Sunday evenings were spent around the radio listening to the favorite comedy and drama programs of the time. Early Christmas mornings we could hardly wait for dawn, so my two brothers and I would always arise about 4 A.M., meet in the bathroom, and sit by the wall heater, hoping morning would soon come so we could line up according to size in front of the living room door, which had been draped with a sheet to conceal what Santa Claus had brought.

Christmas has inspired numerous family customs. For example, families of German descent usually open their presents on Christmas Eve; those of English descent do so on Christmas morning. Christmas customs also vary as to whether a star or an angel is placed atop the tree. Another custom is the reading aloud of the nativity or other favorite Christmas stories or poems. The singing of carols and extra Christmas cooking are yet others.

Birthdays generate similar traditions. One father makes an elaborate ceremony of giving his young children a new silver dollar on their birthdays. A mother presents a door key to her youngsters when they reach sixteen. One family has used the same centerpiece—a large red candle holder—in the birthday cake of every family member for over twenty-five years. Another family awakens a child on his birthday with a music box that sings "Happy Birthday to You!" I know a grandfather who takes each of his grandchildren on a shopping trip on their birthdays to select their own special present.

Then there are many private kinds of family traditions. One father, every Saturday since his daughter's twelfth birthday, takes her to lunch at a fancy restaurant and afterwards to a sporting event, movie, or play. On these special dates, father and daughter never include anyone else, because they discuss the daughter's social feelings, school concerns, and future aspirations.

I remember reading of yet another family which has a regular Saturday night "egg-eating" tradition. It started when their young daughter was in high school and got a summer job to help out the family finances. The first Saturday she worked, she came home late and she and her father fried some eggs and had a pitcher of cold milk. Each Saturday night they ate in the kitchen, talked about their problems and challenges, and put their weekly wages on the table. Then, with the mother of the family, they would plan the expenditures for the coming week. This little custom has continued ever since.

Abraham Lincoln had a family tradition in Springfield. He regularly hauled his sons, Willie and Tad, in a little wagon from home down to his law office. Mary Martin, the actress, says that her household had a secret signal. It consisted of three whistled notes, and the family continues to use it over and over again to greet each other on homecomings—even to locate each other in crowds. John Eisenhower has shared with the public the informal "talking time" he had as a boy with his father, the former general and president. "When my dad shaved, I would just talk to him about anything that was on my mind."

Like customs and traditions, families in every walk of life have enjoyed hobbies, television, home videos, and a host of other activities of every kind and description. What could involve families more than the many amateur sports activities that include boys and girls in Little League sports, track and field events, swimming, soccer, basketball, music, and the many arts and crafts!

But even more popular than any hobby or professional or amateur sports mania is the family reunion. Charles Sprague puts into words the feelings of such a tradition:

> We are all here,
> Father, mother,
> Sister, brother,
> All who hold each other dear.
> Each chair is filled, we are all at home!
> Tonight let no cold stranger come;
> It is not often thus around
> Our old familiar hearth we're found.
> Bless, then, the meeting and the spot,
> For once be every care forgot;
> Let gentle peace assert her power,
> And kind affection rule the hour,
> We're all—all here.
> (*The Home Book of Verse, American and English*, ed. Burton E. Stevenson, 2 vols. [New York: Holt, Rinehart, and Winston, 1953], 2:3562–63.)

Families everywhere in all cultures gather regularly to discover and develop deep, abiding relationships.

Just think for a moment: the earth and everything that is in it belongs to God, and we are mere stewards over what he has placed in our care. Nowhere is that stewardship responsibility so great as with our children, for their spirits exist eternally with ours, and we made the decision to come to earth at the same time they did in that premortal council.

Because of the chronology and order of this earth, and because of many factors that we don't fully understand, we got here twenty or thirty years before they did, and hence, they (our spirit brothers and sisters) came into mortality as our children. Thus they are dependent on us to teach and guide them until they can guide themselves (see D&C 68:25–28).

There is a basic inner draw in all of us to unite with family, to strengthen family ties which we see firmly embedded from the moment of birth. That draw remains in our relationships with family members after death. Even when family relationships are not as ideal as they might be, the feelings of desire for unity are deep and lasting. Consider one family's experience:

"For twelve years my mother lived on alone in their little house with its roses. . . . Then one day when she was eighty-four . . . one bright day after serving lunch for my two brothers who often popped in for a bite and one of their lively debates on how best to improve the world . . . she hung her apron behind the door and went to join God and Dad.

"I wish this were quite as idyllic as it sounds. She had not been feeling well for weeks and I'm sure she sensed that she was going. She had made quite a few little preparations, including leaving instructions, written in her familiar tiny script, in the Bible she always used, on her dresser where we'd be sure to find them.

"But one thing uppermost on her mind she had been able to do little about. There had been a feud in the family. One of those agonizing conflicts between grown children that tear a parent apart. She had wept over it, prayed over it, but the wounds were far from healed.

"But now that the house was silent and we all came rushing back, everybody forgot. People ran sobbing into each other's arms. And there was so much to be done. There was simply no time for hostilities. . . . Yet they refused to vanish altogether even in the face of death. Though proprieties were maintained, even an extra show of courtesy, after that first surge of emotion you could feel them quivering, threatening.

"Then, that second night, we saw her Bible on the coffee table.

"Not the 'new' one given her on some anniversary years ago to replace the heavy, cumbersome old one with its family records. We had already consulted the 'new' one. This was the old one so long ago relegated to the top shelf of the bookcase. Yet here it lay, on a table that had been cleared and dusted several times! Who had gotten it down? . . . Mystified, we consulted each other.

"No one else had been here, at least no one who would have known or cared about that particular Bible. Yet none of us had done so, and each of us was as puzzled as the rest. . . . That Bible simply appeared; there is no other explanation for it.

"Without a word everyone sat down while my sister opened the book at its marker. It opened to the thirteenth chapter of John. In a second she began to read aloud:

" ' "Now before the feast of the Passover, when Jesus knew that his hour was come that he should depart out of this world unto the Father, having loved his own which were in the world, he loved them unto the end." '

"She paused and looked around. All our eyes were wet. Hers went back to the page. 'It goes on to tell the story of how Jesus washed the disciples' feet,' she said. 'And there's this—this place is marked! "Little children, yet a little while I am with you. Ye shall seek me: and as I said unto the Jews, Whither I go, ye cannot come; so now I say to you. A new commandment I give unto you, That ye love one another; as I have loved you, that ye also love one another." '

"She couldn't go on. She didn't have to. The two who had been so tragically separated groped out for each other's hands. Then they embraced, holding each other as if never to let go.

"The peace they made that night was to last. The bridge of death had become the bridge of love that is also God." (From Marjorie Holmes, "Mother's Bible," in *A Marjorie Holmes Treasury: To Help You Through the Hurting,* pp. 66–68. Copyright © 1983 by Marjorie Holmes. Used by permission of Doubleday.)

I wonder what parent would not be willing to leave a marked and open Bible to accomplish what this great mother did! In reality we can.

While all mankind will live again and be resurrected as a result of Christ's atoning sacrifice, not everyone will be exalted. Our belief in the universal application of the Atonement does not mean that all mankind will be saved in like power and glory. The gospel, through the scriptures, gives us the "how to's" of the way back into our Heavenly Father's presence and the procedures by which family members can be reunited.

The Lord has invited all to a heavenly family reunion, and it is my prayer that we make plans to attend.

Not long ago I read a touching story of a young husband and father who discovered, in the midst of a happy, productive, and promising life, that he had an incurable brain tumor and had only a few months to live. Realizing more than ever his great love for his wife and three young children, he decided the best thing he could leave them was part of himself, an account of what was most important to him — what his life meant to him, what he believed in, the special events and feelings he had experienced, his favorite things, and choicest memories. He also expressed his love for and faith in his family members, his words of comfort and advice for their futures. These accounts he put on video tape to give visual remembrance as well as words spoken.

Through the months he had left he struggled courageously and with a will, until finally he knew his time was coming to an end. In a final tape his words were these:

> I know you're fighters. I'm going to be watching over you, because I do believe there is a God. I want you to know that I'll be somewhere, still thinking about you and loving you and waiting for you. . . .
>
> I don't ever want to say good-by, ever. And I don't think I'm going to. Because I'm going to see you again.
>
> Brent, Blair, Blaine. When you feel like you should be holding me, hold your mother. It will be like you're hugging me, because she's half of me. (See Bonnie Remsberg, "I Wish I Could Hold You More," *Reader's Digest,* June 1989, pp. 147– 52.)

We shall live again. We shall also have the blessing of being reunited with our precious loved ones in the kingdom of our Heavenly Father and His Son if we truly "come unto Christ" and follow Him and His teachings.

The plan designed for the fulfillment of that promise was put into effect long ago, the series of all its steps leading to the one ultimate goal, that of the immortality (everlasting life) and eternal life (exaltation) of mankind, both of which glorious blessings are brought about through the atonement of Jesus Christ.

Amulek bore powerful witness to this truth:

> And behold, this is the whole meaning of the law, every whit pointing to that great and last sacrifice; and that great and last sacrifice will be the Son of God, yea, infinite and eternal.
>
> And thus he shall bring salvation [for sin] to all those who shall believe on his name; this being the intent of this last sacrifice, to bring about the bowels of mercy, which overpowereth justice, and bringeth about means unto men that they may have faith unto repentance.
>
> And thus mercy can satisfy the demands of justice, and encircles them in the arms of safety, while he that exercises no faith unto repentance is exposed to the whole law of the demands of justice; therefore only unto him that has faith unto repentance is brought about the great and eternal plan of redemption. (Alma 34:14–16.)

As Christmases come, let us rejoice as we sing:

> Joy to the world, the Lord is come;
> Let earth receive her King!
> Let every heart prepare Him room,
> And Saints and angels sing.
> ("Joy to the World," *Hymns*, no. 201.)

And at Easter let us praise our God through these words:

> He is risen! He is risen!
> Tell it out with joyful voice.
> He has burst His three days' prison;
> Let the whole wide world rejoice.
> ("He Is Risen!" *Hymns*, no. 199.)

May the spirit of these special seasons bear witness to our souls of God's great concern for us, of the truth of the atonement of Jesus Christ, and that our Father could give us no greater gift.

Index